gm+ad

curious rationalism

Edited by Penny Lewis
Introduction by Hugh Pearman

gordon murray + alan dunlop architects

Drummond House
One Hill Street
Glasgow G3 6RN
www.murraydunloparchitects.com

Published by
Carnyx Group Limited
3 Park Street South
Glasgow G3 6BG

ISBN 1-903653-37-1

Photography
All photographs in this book are by Andrew Lee with the exception of the following:
Front cover by Martin Hunter; pages 4 and 20 by Joe Connolly at Simple Photography; images of Clydebank on pages 12 and 68 by Anthony Coleman; page 37 by Paul Hannigan; page 80 by John Glenday (www.futureglasgow.co.uk); image on the right-hand side of page 86 by Russell Davies and page 97 by Brian Sweeney.

The images on page 43 were produced by Ian Denby for Dandara.

Edited by Penny Lewis
Designed by Nick Creed
Imaging and production by Eddie Wright, Fiona McGinn and Jason Byers

Contents

An emerging voice in architecture

By Hugh Pearman

HERE are Gordon Murray and Alan Dunlop, genially ambitious Glasgow architects with a growing office, clearly going places. Their home city is becoming a three-dimensional gallery of their distinctive work. They like to play with your expectations of what a façade should be, for instance – it can sparkle, or glow, or quiver, or even start to peel away completely and become something else, as at the city's Radisson SAS Hotel. They are now working outside Scotland and the UK as well, but the portfolio they are building up north of the Border is consistently interesting. How did they get to this point, where are they headed now, and can you define what they do as somehow rooted here, in the spirit of this place?

It is always difficult to pin down the circumstances that make one architect emerge into the limelight while another may lurk forever in the shadows. Talent is necessary, of course. But talent alone is not enough. A surprising number of architects who have won major national competitions and awards have not continued on into the sunlit uplands of fame and fortune. Some simply cannot handle the pressure, preferring to opt for the quieter, more workaday life of small certainties rather than big competitive gambles. Others have one good project in them – the way some writers have one good novel in them – and never quite manage to get over it. Some get lost in the translation between concept and reality, failing to get to grips with the Byzantine complexities of building for real. Some go mad, some run away. Nobody ever pretended that architecture was easy, though some have the skill to make it seem so.

The best architects acknowledge that their profession is hard, and that it takes time and effort to master. It takes more time still to develop a distinct architectural language or, at a deeper level, what the late Sir Denys Lasdun, architect of the National Theatre, described as a "personal myth". The personal myth is like the source code of a computer operating system. Outsiders cannot see it, but it drives everything you do. The personal myth is essential for an architect's self-belief because it enables him or her to feel superior to the opposition. The best architects may well admire the work of others, but they have to feel they could always do as well or better. It is what makes architects, in my experience, fiercely partisan critics. No quarter is given, none expected, when architects lock horns over each others' work. Those of a nervous disposition should look away.

Beyond all this is the unknowable hand of fate. Some architects just find themselves in the right place at the right time – economically and geographically – and so find outlets for their design skills. This is crucial because the civic realm never develops smoothly, but in fits and starts. Every city has its golden periods, interspersed with longeurs. History is as littered with good architects who deserved to build more in bad times, as it is with lesser architects who somehow got too much of the cake during booms.

Put all this together – thus yielding the desirable happy conjunction of the planets – and you have the conditions in which architecturally fruitful things can start to happen. This is where the history of Gordon Murray and Alan Dunlop dovetails with the broader history of British regional architecture in the 'things can only get better' era.

That naff pop song/political slogan was absolutely correct. Things could only get better. From the mid-1990s onwards, as the British economy pulled itself out of a trough, a new generation of architects started to build. Just as we used to be told in school that the Great Fire of London cleansed the capital of bubonic plague (wrongly – the 1665 plague had abated before the 1666 fire) so you could argue that the recession of the early 1990s had sounded the death-knell of decadent postmodernism. Well, maybe, and maybe it had run its course anyway. Whatever, the architects who started to get noticed as building recommenced generally went back to the mother lode of modernism to recharge their personal-myth drives. This time round, there was more scope for variation.

I won't dwell here on the history of the practice that became gm+ad. You can trace its roots back to 1931, its personnel changing though the generations. The point is that around the time it assumed its present name and form in 1999, architecture in Scotland was in one of its interesting phases. Glasgow was successfully making the transition to a post-industrial economy; not without hiccups and mistakes, but the will was there and increasingly the buildings as well. 1999 was the Year of Architecture and Design, awarded to Glasgow in recognition of the strides it had already made. Meanwhile, Edinburgh was starting to wake up. At one point Auld Reekie had become so paralysed by doubt about what and where to build that the city centre had become virtually a no-go area for progressive architects, patrolled as it was by militant conservationists. That had started to change, though not always for the better, in the late 1980s. By the late 1990s, however, Edinburgh was galvanised both by a burgeoning commercial sector – the Richard Meier-master planned Edinburgh Park, for instance, where gm+ad has contributed a building – and by its position as capital of the newly devolved and long-wished-for Scottish Parliament. Where power goes, money follows, and money means buildings.

This being the case then, it is very significant that the first project to bring gm+ad to national and international attention was very high profile indeed: its involvement with leading Australian architects Denton Corker Marshall for the Scottish Parliament building at Holyrood. Technically, this – which made it to the final shortlist of five exalted international names – was one of the last projects of the practice under its former name of Glass Murray. It is tempting, and fruitless, to speculate how things might have turned out had the competition dice fallen differently, if the proposed big ellipse of a debating chamber had come to dominate the familiar site. But we know the winner, and how controversial and expensive – and wonderful but wilful – it became. Arguably gm+ad was well out of that process, which was as predictably messy at the foot of the Royal Mile as it is with just about every other seemingly gilt-edged British public building project. It would in any case have been doomed to a lifetime of arguing over its place in the credits, an occupational hazard of all such joint ventures.

I think that the Scottish Parliament competition served the practice well; it whetted the appetite, sharpened its ambition, provided it with an outlook beyond the parish boundaries. International collaboration and competition at this level is invaluable, but consider also the sheer chutzpah of a Glasgow practice being allowed anywhere near Edinburgh's most symbolically important building.

Certainly it is from that point onwards that you can detect a new confidence and desire for formal experimentation in the work of the practice, something that mirrors the path that Scotland itself was taking, compared with its sister nation across the Border. At the same time, it is important to remember that around the United Kingdom as a whole, regional cities were and are reviving fast – to begin with, faster than London. Manchester led the way with its post-bomb reconstruction, but architects of note were also emerging in Liverpool and Leeds, Birmingham and Bath, inner cities and rural shires.

Equally important is the architectural dialogue happening between Scotland and Ireland, where economic growth has been continuous for much longer than in the UK. The community of architects in Dublin, for instance, share certain ideals with their Scottish counterparts, such as the establishment of a definable modern architecture of place that does not depend on the crumbs falling from the stylistic tables of London, Chicago or Rotterdam. All architecture is international in the way influences are disseminated and absorbed, but that does not stand in the way of what the critic Colin Rowe called "critical regionalism", which he also defined as an "architecture of resistance". Resistance to what? Resistance to sameness, to cookie-cutter global style.

Having said that, you can no more brand the work of gm+ad as specifically Scottish than you could the work of Robert Adam, Basil Spence or John McAslan, say – all Scottish architects who migrated south. Charles Rennie Mackintosh's little 1916 house in Northampton is a piece of late Mackintosh, not a piece of displaced fin-de-siecle Glasgow. It comes as no surprise to find gm+ad working on a project in Sligo, Ireland, nor that it has done studies for hotels in English cities. I would expect to find it building in England and elsewhere before too long.

So what can one identify in its approach? Perhaps a certain vigour that is more industrial, shipbuilding Glasgow than administrative, white-collar Edinburgh. There is a hint of plated hulls in some of its work. Then there is the disciplining geometry of the Glasgow grid-plan, which seems to find an echo in the sharp-edged rectilinear buildings the practice produces, such as the award-winning Sentinel office building with its night-time light show. But then you have to add in the fact that it likes to disrupt things a little, serrate a façade or pull it apart or give it a peaked cap, as at the Bewley's Hotel. There's a bit of welcome mischief in what it does. Perhaps its personal myth is subversion. People tend to argue about its buildings. Is that a Glasgow thing? Are you looking at me?

It has been said by others, and they're right, that gm+ad manages to comfortably work in the commercial and public worlds simultaneously. This is a signifier of a good architect because it means someone who rejects typecasting and applies no formula. There is no reason for an office building or a hotel to look anything like a special-needs school, let alone a bridge. This may seem obvious, but I know several new schools by leading architects that are exactly like blocks in a business park. This is some contrast with the competition-winning Dumbreck Special School – an organically inspired, embracing place. Equally, the practice has got onto shortlists against illustrious opposition for imaginative new bridges in both Glasgow and Cardiff. It can design a little artists' retreat on Loch Fyne, while simultaneously producing what amounts to an entire high-rise city district at Glasgow Harbour.

It got to this point not by suddenly emerging from college with any extreme manifesto position or influential patron or membership of the 'signature architects' magic circle, but by working separately at its craft, developing its skills, joining forces at the right time, and having good ideas. I get the impression that there is also a useful creative tension between the older and the younger man, between experience and impulsiveness, that benefits both. Certainly it is a very self-aware practice, active in the UK politics of its profession and – something I know from direct experience, having collaborated with it on a project – conscious of the need for the best regional architects to have more of a voice.

This is important because the UK, unlike other European nations, concentrates so much of its architectural resource base in the capital. Given the economic power of London this is hardly surprising, but it can cast a shadow across the rest of the country. We need to develop a situation more like Germany, where the best architects are as likely to be found in Hamburg or Stuttgart as Berlin; or Portugal, where Oporto boasts more important architects than Lisbon; or above all Spain, where such a renaissance is happening all over that it became the subject of a major exhibition at New York's Museum of Modern Art early in 2006.

There are signs that things are changing in the UK, with the best regional architects starting to compete on equal terms with some of their London and overseas colleagues. Scotland, which always had an independent tradition in British architecture, is reinforcing that identity following devolution, though there are still plenty of London architects very active north of the Border. In a just world, Gordon Murray and Alan Dunlop, along with several others from the Scottish architectural community, would do far more work down south. They are certainly entering some of the key competitions now and getting onto shortlists, so it is only a matter of time. In the past, you had to up sticks and essentially emigrate south to make your mark. Today, that should not be necessary, especially with all the openings now available in Scotland itself.

So gm+ad is living in interesting times in the best sense, and this is a good moment to be writing about it. I certainly cannot make any predictions as to what it will find itself doing, or where, in five or ten years' time. The architectural fates work in mysterious ways. But to judge by the pattern established so far, we can expect a bigger, more diverse, more geographically spread workload including – I would hope – some intriguing landmark buildings including bridges. It is certainly possible to argue that it represents a can-do Glasgow attitude. In which case, I would want that to be an exportable commodity.

Hugh Pearman is architecture and design critic of the Sunday Times, London, and author of several books including Contemporary World Architecture, published by Phaidon.

Essay

By Penny Lewis

IT'S ten years since Gordon Murray and Alan Dunlop began their partnership. During that time the practice has developed significantly. While in the Nineties they were pigeonholed as 'commercial architects', they now have a broad range of commissions including a school for visually and sensory impaired children, a 700-home development on the banks of the Clyde and a scheme for the redevelopment of the historic centre of Sligo. The commission for the school in the suburbs of Glasgow is significant for gm+ad. "Hazelwood School potentially takes us in a different direction," says Dunlop. It takes the practice into the public sector and allows it to bury a stereotype, the idea that it only produces aggressive buildings on hard-nosed city centre sites.

All architects like to work across development sectors, but gm+ad's efforts to break out of the commercial sector represent something more than risk management. It's an expression of its energy and its desire to extend its reach beyond Glasgow and Scotland. In the past ten years the practice has worked on 433 projects, six open competitions and 15 invited ones and has won 230 commissions. So far, 38 of those commissions have been built. The office employs architects with a wide range of experience from the UK, Germany, Spain, China, Ireland and America. It has developed a studio that is design-led but has a strong sensitivity to the commercial interests of its clients and the practice.

Ever since local authorities architects' departments disappeared in the 1980s, the architectural profession in Scotland has been divided into two camps. On the one hand are the large established practices driven by managers; on the other side are the smaller practices in which the partners lead the design process and often sustain their income and enthusiasm by teaching. In the 1990s the design-led practices benefited from publicly funded work while business-led practices serviced the private sector. More recently, the arrival of PPP and the growth in urban private residential developments has confused these allegiances. gm+ad now finds itself in the unusual position of straddling both camps – design-led and business-led – in the professional divide at a time when the precise role and status of the architect is shifting.

Murray and Dunlop now embark on their second decade in partnership with a strong sense of purpose. The buildings that the practice is currently producing have a common sense of conviction rather than a set of recognisable details or a house style. "No two buildings that we do are the same," says Murray. The practice operates on the principle that it is worth exploring new possibilities and taking risks, particularly with the use of materials and colour. Visiting the Radisson SAS Hotel and the Clydebank workshops it is hard to believe that the highly expressive building in Glasgow and the restrained boxes in Clydebank are produced by the same office. But if you look closer you can see a consistency in the flat flush façade on the courtyard of the Radisson and John Knox Street. And there is a link between the playful approach to decoration and colour on the Clydebank sheds and the vivid green of the hotel's copper façade. The work produced by the office is not eclectic or disparate; it is just very open. Each building is part of an unfolding process.

As a practice it is hard to define the character of gm+ad. Although strongly influenced by modernism, particularly American modernism, it doesn't produce 'Mac-modernism'. Its commercial buildings are devoid of that slightly apologetic character often exhibited in many of Britain's speculative offices. The lobby of the Sentinel Building opens up to and engages with the street with a sense of self-assurance that echoes the lobbies of the work of Ludwig Mies Van der Rohe, and the early work of SOM. The pared-down structure and careful detailing stems from an engagement with the same tradition.

Its buildings are often playful, decorative and occasional symbolic, but are not postmodern. When it comes to the programme and the planning of the building, gm+ad is much closer to Le Corbusier than Alsop. There is a strong strand of the Swiss-cum-Dutch fascination with surface in its work. But the Dutch wouldn't like the exuberant expressionism in some of the projects, which have more in common with the work of Louis Kahn or James Stirling than they do with contemporary form-makers such as Zaha Hadid.

Murray has a particular interest in the work of James Stirling; he enjoys poetry and allegory and he likes the idea of reading things in the building. They both want to create buildings that demonstrate a depth of thinking, but they are not the kind of architects that carry around ready-made stories about the origin of a building concept or wear their visual metaphors on their sleeve. Dunlop is interested in creating drama and he gets particularly animated when talking about colour.

One of the most distinctive features of the practice's work is its ability to hold on to an idea and retain the capacity to influence the outcome of the construction process, regardless of the procurement method. Sentinel epitomises this approach; the £10 million speculative office development on the edge of Glasgow's financial centre is a robust and legible building. It is commercial – gm+ad understands how to put something together that works for the developer – but at the same time, the design is driven by a strong idea, a simple diagram of geometries and functions that grew out of the needs of the client and the surrounding urban fabric.

The practice is very interested in detail, but doesn't seem to share the British obsession with it. Detailing is not seen as an opportunity to craft the intimate corners of the building, to create a gratifying shadow gap or a timber reveal, but to pare things down, to preserve the clarity of the original conceptual idea. I once attended a lecture by Dunlop at the Mackintosh School of Architecture. During the question time a student asked why the practice had not built the pilotti supporting the copper façade at the Radisson with concrete, but had chosen to build in steel and box the columns in to look like cast concrete. Unperturbed, Dunlop explained that the concept of structural integrity is far less important to him than creating a building of interest. This attitude challenges a strongly held sentiment within the profession, and among academia, that serious architects don't ever make such compromises.

Both partners have publicly expressed concerns about PPP procurement but gm+ad is not afraid of new procurement methods. There is a robustness to the way the practice operates; you could describe it as old-fashioned, in a profession where architects increasingly throw their hands in the air and say, 'What could I do, it was beyond my control!' This confidence stems from employing staff with a range of experience and a belief – a rather old-fashioned but admirable belief – in the role of the architect as the leader of the design and construction process.

In the past the practice was accused of producing false icons, of creating buildings that are dominated by exuberant architectural gestures, or one-liners, which should be understood as marketing rather than architecture. There are some clever simple moves in the office's portfolio, but these design decisions are not 'freebies' slapped on to mediocre buildings to cheer them up. Creating evocative buildings is an integral part of the practice's design intentions.

In the 1990s gm+ad's work looked a bit out of place in Scotland, but things are changing. For the last two decades of the 20th century, architects working in Scotland developed a particular architectural language; you could call it polite modernism or even critical regionalism. Much of the best work produced was underpinned by a handful of basic assumptions: the height of the average tenement was understood as the most appropriate measure for the height of contemporary buildings; indigenous materials, vernacular forms and traditional construction were best privileged over industrial products and imports; and a white render was ubiquitous. In this context it is easy to see why excessively large projecting eaves (Bewleys), rippling aluminium cladding (Spectrum) and mega copper walls (Radisson) were not received with universal enthusiasm.

In the *Architectural Review* (February 2002) Murray responded to a debate on critical regionalism with a clear statement. "Architecture is no longer at the mercy of a specific economy, topography or climate. Even Ken Yang is exportable" – a reference to the fact that Yang himself represents a localised Asian response to modernism. Murray went on to say that architects working in Porto have more in common with their contemporaries in Glasgow or Dublin than they do with the architects that created Porto. This belief is clearly expressed in the practice's portfolio.

Although the influences on gm+ad are international, and it rejects the dogma of Scottish modernism, Murray and Dunlop view themselves as contextualist. "The most important thing to me is site and context," says Dunlop. "Our work is not contextual in the sense that it has to fit in with the surroundings. It is contextual in that it is created at a point in time."

It has a strong appreciation of Scotland's built heritage and argues that all of its buildings are a product of both place and time. Murray and Dunlop embrace Rafael Moneo's description of the process of working with the urban grain of the city. Moneo has often drawn parallels between working with the grid and playing a hand of poker. He rejected the idea of a definitive theory of urban form. "The city is not predetermined, it is open. And yet the pertinence of what exists already will come to bear no matter what the architect does," he said (RIBA Gold Medal speech 2003). "You can never go back to the beginning; you always have to move forward," is Murray's take on the question.

The practice seems to understand scale. The two projects featured at the front of this book, Hazelwood School and Glasgow Harbour Phase 2, both have difficult sites and both design solutions are a product of their setting. Hazelwood is sensitively handled; it is built of timber and slate and hugs the land and embraces the landscape. Glasgow Harbour may look bullish, but it is an equally sensitive response.

At Glasgow Harbour the practice has designed a scheme with a scale and density that appears to match post-war comprehensive development. To break from the original Kohn Pedersen Fox master plan was a brave move; to have accepted the old framework would have meant abdicating responsibility for an important chunk of the city. gm+ad's harbour plans are an appropriate response to the scale of the place, but they are put forward in a culture where we find high-density, large-scale development a bit alien, where we only really feel comfortable with piecemeal insertions that mimic the historic fabric as we imagine it to be. This sentiment is culturally specific, a product of our cautious and risk-averse culture. gm+ad is not oblivious to contemporary preoccupations, but sets out to challenge them, because it believes that higher densities are essential to maintain the critical mass of a shrinking city.

As Jonathan Glancey says, gm+ad has "a view to the future". The partners' confidence in the future seems to come from a solid understanding of the recent past.

Both Murray and Dunlop are big Ludwig Mies van der Rohe enthusiasts. On his return from a recent trip to Chicago Alan Dunlop sounded uncharacteristically like a conservationist. He was enraged about the negative impact of the new Trump Tower on views of the façade of Mies' IBM building.

Murray is a visiting professor at the Strathclyde University. He has pushed forward a programme for final year students to rework Cumbernauld, Scotland's most ambitious megastructure. Unlike so many other architects of his generation, Murray is not defensive about the post-war output of the profession. In an article on Cumbernauld in *Architectural Digest* published in February 2006, Murray described how the original intentions of the scheme were based on a long-term rationale to create a modern adaptable city. "Cumbernauld was never allowed to develop that rationale. Instead it was measured against the crude mechanics of 1970s retail theory and found wanting. The clarity of the idea is now lost in a series of corrosive interventions," he wrote.

The strength of the practice lies in the partnership between Murray and Dunlop. They talk about a 'depth of knowledge' provided by the experienced architects in the office as the basis on which they are able to innovate. The office is structured to ensure that younger architects get plenty of experience and more experienced architects are given space to operate. Both partners have an eye on the long-term future of the practice because they are passionate and committed to their discipline and they have the confidence to plot a course for the future.

Penny Lewis is editor of Prospect, the Scottish architecture magazine. She has written widely for national newspapers and magazines and is a member of the Saltire Housing Panel.

289B
289A

Public work

An interview with Alan Dunlop

WHEN gm+ad won the competition for Hazelwood School in summer 2003 it meant more to the practice than a single commission. It was its first opportunity to show what it could do in the public sector. "It was not only a new type of project for us, it was also new for Glasgow City Council and they clearly want it to be an exemplary building," says Dunlop. Construction has begun and should be completed by Easter 2007.

The project is located outside of Glasgow city centre in Dumbreck on the city's Southside. Glasgow City Council had used PPP procurement for its last school building programme, but had decided to build its next nine schools under a traditional contract. gm+ad responded to an OJEU notice and was shortlisted. "We were desperate to get other types of work, to break away from the label 'commercial architects'. We normally get on shortlists for this kind of job, only to be told that we didn't win because we don't have the right experience," recalls Dunlop. Fortunately the practice had a very positive reference from Keir Bloomer at Clackmannanshire Council, which they had been working for, along with Richard Murphy and Gareth Hoskins, on possible design proposals for a school in Alloa.

The school will cater for 52 children between the ages of four and 18. Most of the children have dual sensory impairment; they are deaf and blind or blind and physically handicapped, and a few are partially sighted. When gm+ad was looking for literature on this particular building type, it found little on designing for the blind but there was even less on designing for children with dual sensory impairment. So it has been working from first principles and recognises that the fine-tuning of the design of the building will be a case of trial and error and that even once it is completed some things will need to be changed.

"Our fundamental aim is to create a secure space in which the children were able to play and learn independently," explains Dunlop. The philosophy was not to make everything too safe, to ensure that the children were challenged. Dunlop was also keen to ensure that they were providing a very pleasant place to work for staff and a reassuring environment that would make it easier for parents to leave their vulnerable children in the school's care. "We wanted to create somewhere that would put parents and pupils at ease, somewhere that didn't feel too institutional. And we wanted to design somewhere where the carers are not always sitting on the children's shoulders, where they have freedom, but are never put at risk."

gm+ad spent 14 months in consultation with the

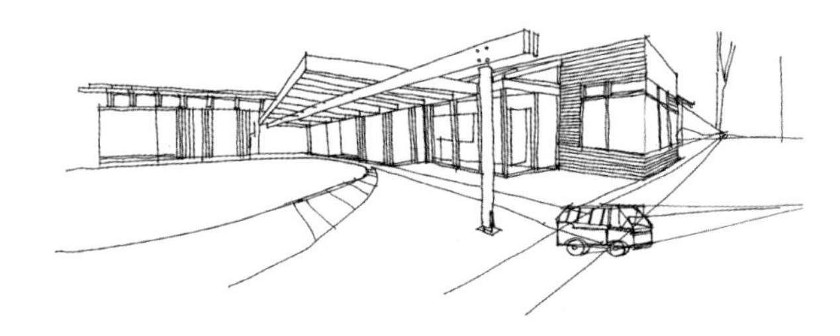

Early sketch showing the entrance and presentation drawing showing the south-facing court organised around existing beech trees.

The school, which is built on a wooded site, sits beneath the tree line.

Elevations showing the school in context. North, south, section and east

RNIB, Yorkhill Hospital and Professor Gordon Dutton, an ophthalmic specialist, gathering information and reviewing the impact of its design decisions. The difficulties faced by the children made the design process very challenging. "If you looked at all of the possible difficulties a child might have, you could never make a mark on the page," admits Dunlop. "What was clear was that this new building needed to have plenty of visual and tactile clues for the children to use to orientate themselves." In response to this, gm+ad developed the idea of a sensory wall, a spine that ran right through the building that would contain tactile messages that allowed the children to orientate themselves. The wall is covered in cork and is faceted, it snakes along the centre of the building, with rails and grooves at various heights for different ages of children. It also doubles as a storage wall, a very important resource for a school that has large pieces of children's play equipment.

The history of the site Hazelwood is interesting. It sits on the edge of a conservation area, close to Bellahouston Park. Like most Glasgow parks, it is edged by old lime trees but in the centre are three large beech trees that date from about 1915. The site was originally used as a dairy, but it was demolished in the late 1920s and the residents of Torridon Avenue, the next street, had been looking at green space ever since, so the city council knew any development would be contentious. The planning process took about nine months. It was referred to the Scottish Executive, mainly because the city was both the applicant and the planning authority, and after 28 days the Executive gave the project the go-ahead.

"We were keen to make as much use as possible of the natural landforms," says Dunlop. "We have been working closely with Richard East, the landscape designer from City Design Co-op. He played a fundamental role from a very early stage, making sure that the building works with the existing landscape and creating a secure environment for the children. We made the decision to create a building that would wind its way around the central beeches; we have retained every tree on the site."

The building is long and thin and it curves around the trees. Inside, a street forms a route along the building with classrooms to the north and doors onto the garden spaces to the south. The section is simple; the roof tilts up to the north to capture extra light. In the northern wall there are storytelling seats and doors out to independent exterior spaces where children can go and let off steam. To the south, the roofline extends 1.8 metres beyond the building to create a shaded area in the garden.

There are 11 classrooms with moveable partitions. Teaching is organised on a one-to-one basis with about ten children and ten staff in each room. The education is

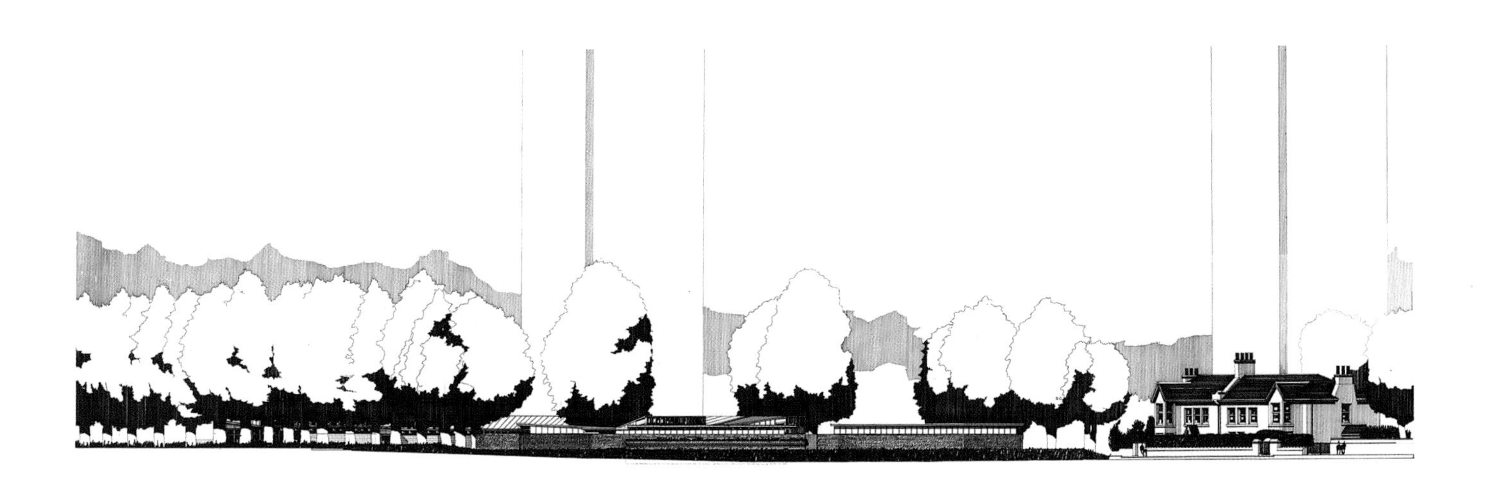

gm+ad

Hazelwood loops its way around the existing trees. Sketches made during the early stages of the project.

often quite physical, with teachers helping the children use their sense of touch and hearing to develop life skills.

The entrance area and pool can be closed off from the rest of the school at night, which means that the school resource could be used by the local community and for school events. The children at the school vary in age from four to 18 and the aim of the school is to ensure that they can play as big a part in the community as they possibly can. The arrangement of age groups through the school reflects this; the youngest children are located near the door and at the far end of the building is a separate space for 16 to 18-year-olds. The section of the school for older children is separated from the rest of the school by a light glass roof. Beside the entrance there is a hydrotherapy hall and dining area. On the north-east corner of the site there will be a three-bedroom life-skills residential unit where older students can stay overnight and test their ability to operate independently. Glasgow City Council wants the centre to become a centre of excellence for this type of education and so there is also a room for visitors.

"We wanted to make a timber building, because it is tactile, it smells nice and people enjoy timber. We decided to expose the timber structure and make something of it," says Dunlop. "We also thought it would sit comfortably in the landscape; the timber would age alongside the surrounding buildings, so that in 20 years' time the trees and the timber cladding would be indistinguishable." gm+ad also wanted the building to be rough and shallow and to hug the ground. It picked zinc for the roof's shallow pitches, which will weather and pick up the colour of the sky, and it selected vertically hung slate, a material that it has used in a different form on a number of its buildings.

"When we started by looking at colour we put on sight inhibitors and stumbled around to see what difference colours made to partially sighted children. It is conventional for this type of scheme for architects to use candy colours, but we found that subtle colours did not register," says Dunlop. The practice visited a similar school in Italy, which was finished in pastel colours, but learned that where there was no clear contrast, the partially sighted children couldn't use colour to orientate themselves. As a result, it picked out strong blocks of autumnal colours, such as ochre, olive and beech, to decorate the building.

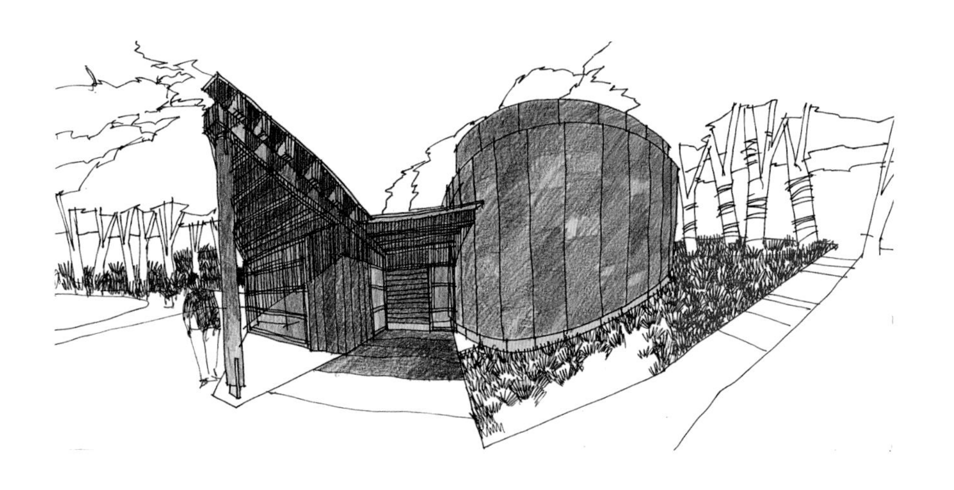

DUMBRECK PLACE
DUMBRECK COURT
TORRIDON AVENUE
TORRIDON AVENUE
DUMBRECK ROAD
FLEURS AVENUE
MOSSPARK BOULEVARD

Plan of Dumbreck area showing surrounding residential development.

Site plan showing the ground-floor plan
1. Entrance
2. Admin
3. Pool
4. Storage wall
5. Classroom
6. Senior School
7 Life Skills House

Model of building demonstrating roof structure.

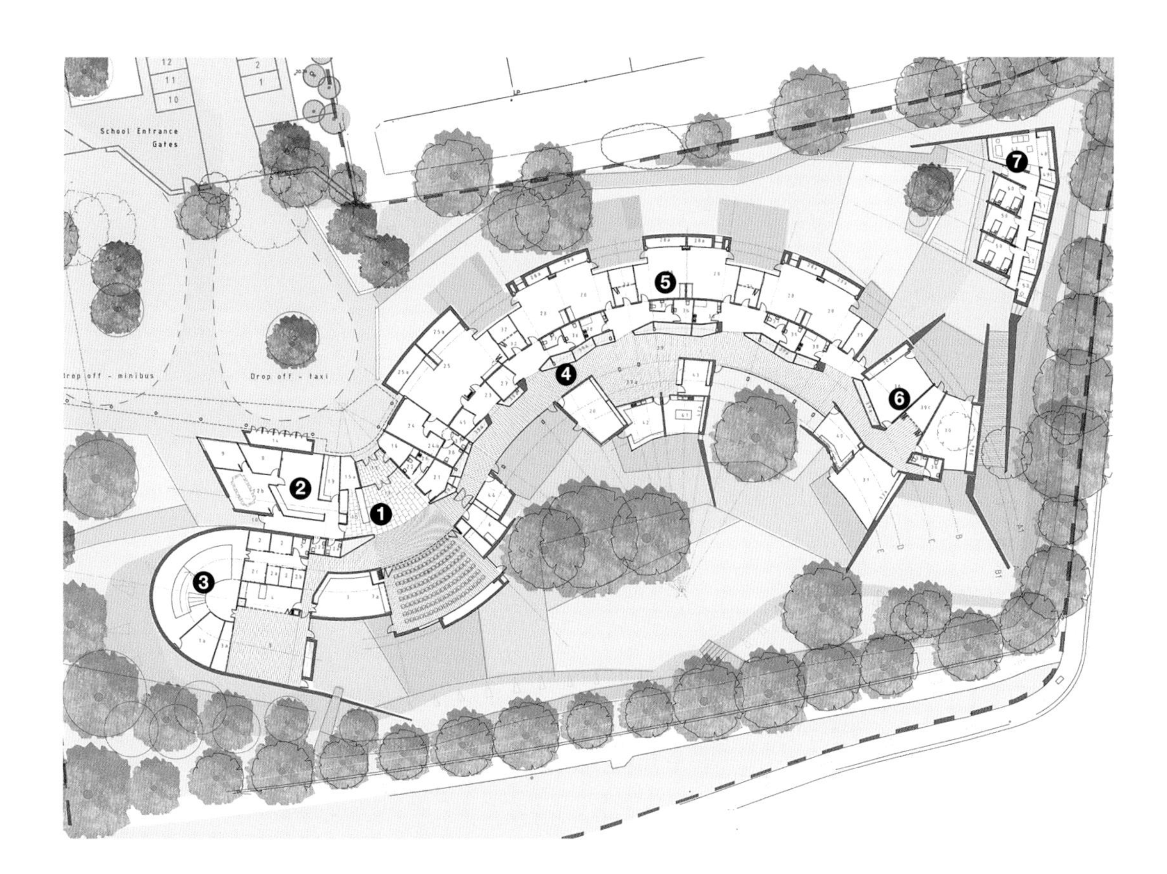

North elevation showing the vertical slate wall.

North elevation of classrooms.

"Our fundamental aim is to create a secure space in which the children are able to play and learn independently. The philosophy was not to make everything too safe, we were asked to ensure that there was a challenge in everything. We also recognised that it is difficult for carers and teachers working with the children and we wanted to create the best possible environment for them." Alan Dunlop

The school street and the garden area beyond.

The interior showing the cork wall, designed as a datum that can be used by the children to orientate themselves within the school.

Reminders produced within the office to help the design process following an investigation of the sensory abilities of the children.

Early sketch showing the courtyard.

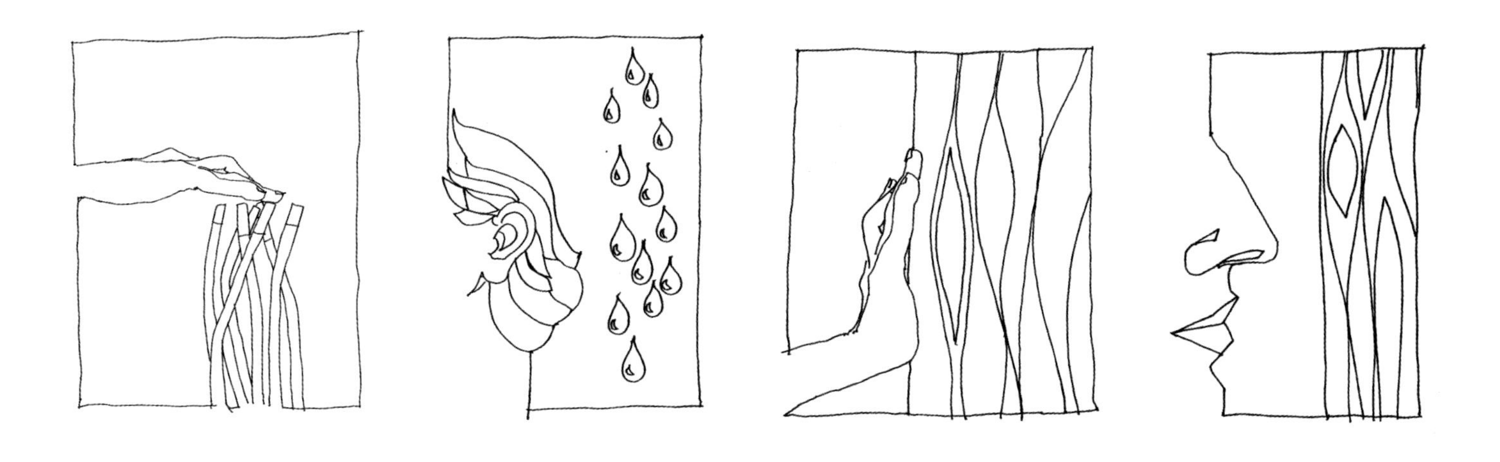

Scale and density

An interview with Gordon Murray

"HONG Kong was the most efficient city in the world and Detroit was the least," says Gordon Murray. He is not concerned in absolute terms about a growing ecological footprint, but he does want to see cities, in particular Glasgow, growing. "Of course there are people that say that cities like Glasgow are shrinking and we should build accommodation that matches that shift. I think that it is important that we structure our economies and create the mechanics to ensure that population does increase. If the population drops below a certain level you have a real problem. The dynamic of a city demands a certain population; there is a figure below which certain things that you associate with a city no longer happen.

"If cities are to be sustainable then they need a critical mass of population, they need to re-densify. If you don't have a critical mass you lose out on work and leisure," he adds. He is visibly frustrated by the suggestion that the new plans for Glasgow Harbour are described as 'too big'. gm+ad has never been afraid of dealing with scale and is always prepared to challenge prevailing orthodoxies. When it was first asked to look at the Glasgow Harbour site, the second phase of a master plan drawn up by Kohn Pederson Fox in the 1990s, it knew that it was going to have to radically review the proposed layout. "The densities achieved during the 20th century are far lower than previous centuries. The RIBA/Egan Review, Delivering Quality with Quantity, suggests a minimum density of 80-100 homes per hectare, which should be compared with central Paris at 300 units/h or Barcelona at 500 units/h. If similar densities were applied to Glasgow, its population of about 600,000 could be housed in 1,200 hectares. In this respect the tenement form is, in some areas, inappropriate for achieving higher densities."

When gm+ad first released images of the plans for Glasgow Harbour, there were complaints. In the media its tall blocks were compared to the Red Road flats, the notorious high-rise slum towers to the north of the city. "They use Red Road because it is pejorative, short-hand for everything that is wrong with high-rise living. But not all high-rise blocks are a failure. The housing scheme just across the road from our office is very successful. It has a controlled mixed tenure, deck access and a simple architecture of its time with landscaping and shared facilities like the bowling green. In the 1960s and 70s a lot of the problems with tall blocks derived from the new technology. We are now in a much better position; we have a much more sophisticated understanding of construction and materials and a sharper awareness of the issues at ground level."

Developer Dandara embarked on Glasgow Harbour

The site for Glasgow Harbour Phase 2 was previously occupied by the Meadowside granaries. Opposite, on the other side of the Clyde, the Govan shipyard continues to produce and repair large boats.

Phase 2 at a time when there was a flurry of media reports about the over-supply of new homes in the Glasgow market. However, the developer knows both the market and its product very well. gm+ad is designing affordable flats that could make Clydeside living a much more appealing proposition for first-time buyers.

gm+ad won the commission for Glasgow Harbour Phase 2 in summer 2004 and by the autumn had lodged the planning application. In February 2005 it received planning permission and the project is now on site. It involves the construction of 700 new homes, which will be built in a rolling programme of three phases to be completed by 2010. The site, which sits at the bend in the river offering oblique views of the site from both banks, used to be occupied by old granaries, and has been cleared ready for new work to begin.

The client is Dandara, the Manchester-based residential developer. Dandara ranks alongside Urban Splash as the most significant clients commissioning contemporary new homes in Northern cities of the UK. It has its own contracting wing and its own R&D wing that looks at ergonomics and psychology. It gathers feedback from everything it builds and uses it to refine the next development. "For Dandara nothing is left to chance; every detail is thought through. We sit as part of a review group that looks at the development of the flat design. The research and development wing of Dandara also looks at construction. They believe that there is no point building above about 22 or 23 floors because you need to embark on a different kind of construction unless the price of floor space is considerably higher. They are aiming at a market that is affordable.

"It would have been easy, when taking on this job, to have opted for the conservative options, to have designed units that sat on the footprints of the buildings designed by KPF, but to build taller doughnut-shaped blocks."

The first phase of the Kohn Pedersen Fox master plan, which is recently completed, follows this pattern. "We were concerned that in the first phase of the development, there were internal courts that didn't get sunlight. That is not always a problem; it's OK with a four-storey tenemental block, but in these taller blocks it might become a problem. David Mackay of MBM also talks about designing beside water and the importance of building at 90 degrees to the river."

For the last two decades the tenement form of development has undergone something of a revival in Glasgow – and there is a lot that can be learned from tenements about the control of light, good space-planning and the relationship between private, semi-private and public space. However, the result is that the form has had something of a stranglehold on the imagination of many

gm+ad's proposals for Glasgow Harbour Phase 2 deliberately challenged the original KPF master plan which proposed doughnut-shaped accommodation occupying the river façade. gm+ad proposes taller blocks and a more open master plan to allow the penetration of light into the site. They have thought carefully about the consequences of this approach at ground level.

leading architects and planners. Conversely, gm+ad thinks the tenement form is inappropriate beside the Clyde. And visiting the area with its old warehouses and cranes, its position seems very rational. "There is this idea that you should replicate the tenement form at Glasgow Harbour, but I don't think it was right for that part of town. It's a question of scale in relation to the river Clyde; the Clyde supports taller buildings of greater mass. Glasgow Harbour Phase 2 is an extension to the city, not a continuation of the West End suburban form," explains Murray. But Murray is no philistine. The practice developed a plan that consists of five towers set at 90 degrees to the water and a line of lower terraces to the north of the site where the development stretches out towards the existing West End tenements at Partick. He talks very eloquently about the grain of this part of the city and the way in which the old industrial sheds and the roads often frame long vistas across the river towards the Ayrshire hills. "It was important that this connectivity was not lost," he says.

"We looked at various different ways of organising the units. We tried placing them at 45 degrees, producing Alvar Aalto-like fans. By placing the towers on a north-south axis we can maximise daylight into the heart of the site whilst providing a river view for the majority of occupants."

The Dandara is primarily a residential developer, but the proposal includes some commercial spaces, which open onto public terraces and squares. Between the public squares and the bases of the taller buildings are a series of private and enclosed garden spaces.

In order to minimise the edges of the towers, enhancing their slenderness, the blocks are halved and dislocated in a horizontal and vertical shift further reinforced by the use of two materials. Similarly, in order to produce a rhythm within the façade design, double height vertical elements are overlaid onto horizontal elements. The building blocks, the basic components, glazed ceramic panels and copper sheeting, are appropriately scaled to allude to massive ashlar dimension or large steel plates of ships' hulls.

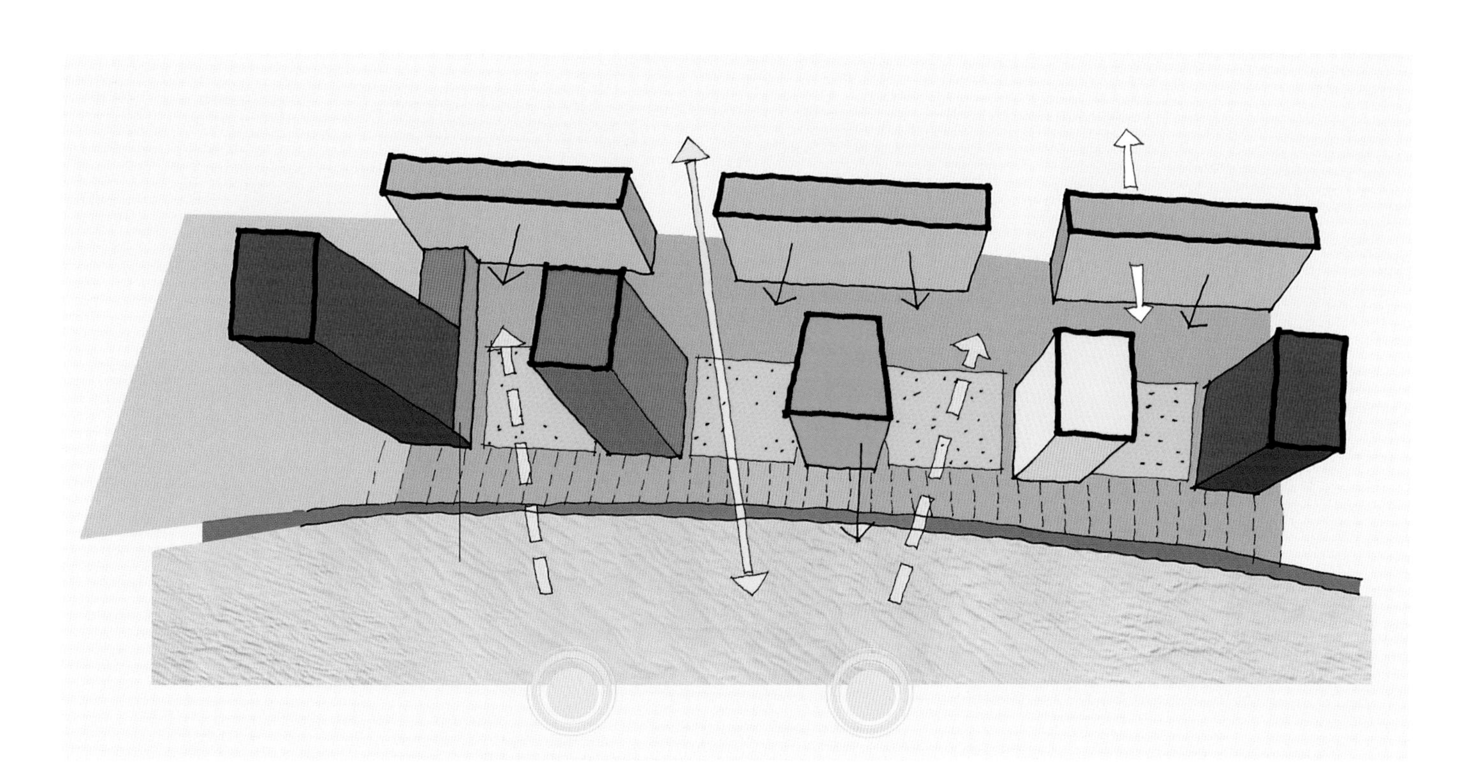

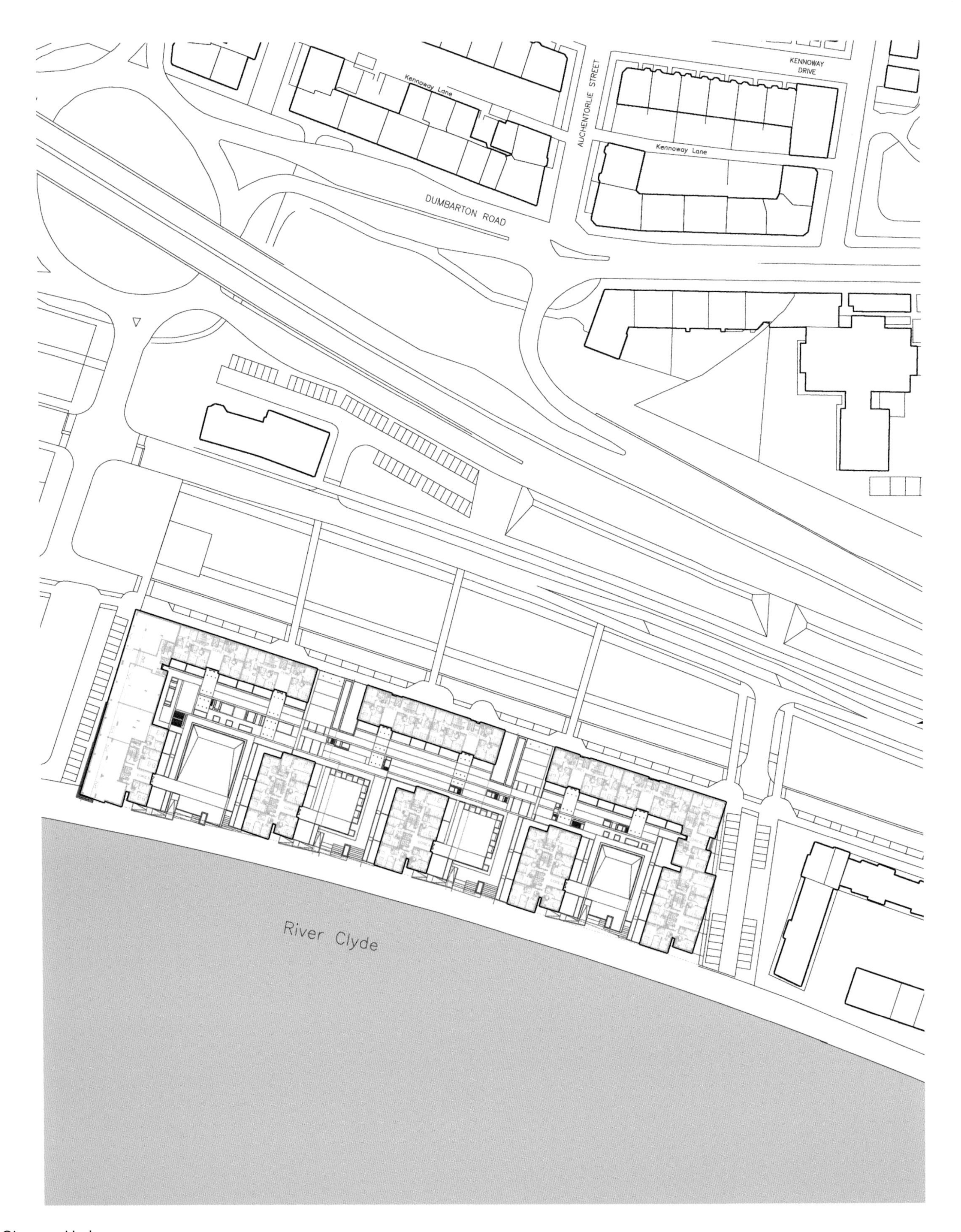
Kennoway Lane
AUCHENTORLIE STREET
KENNOWAY DRIVE
Kennoway Lane
DUMBARTON ROAD
River Clyde

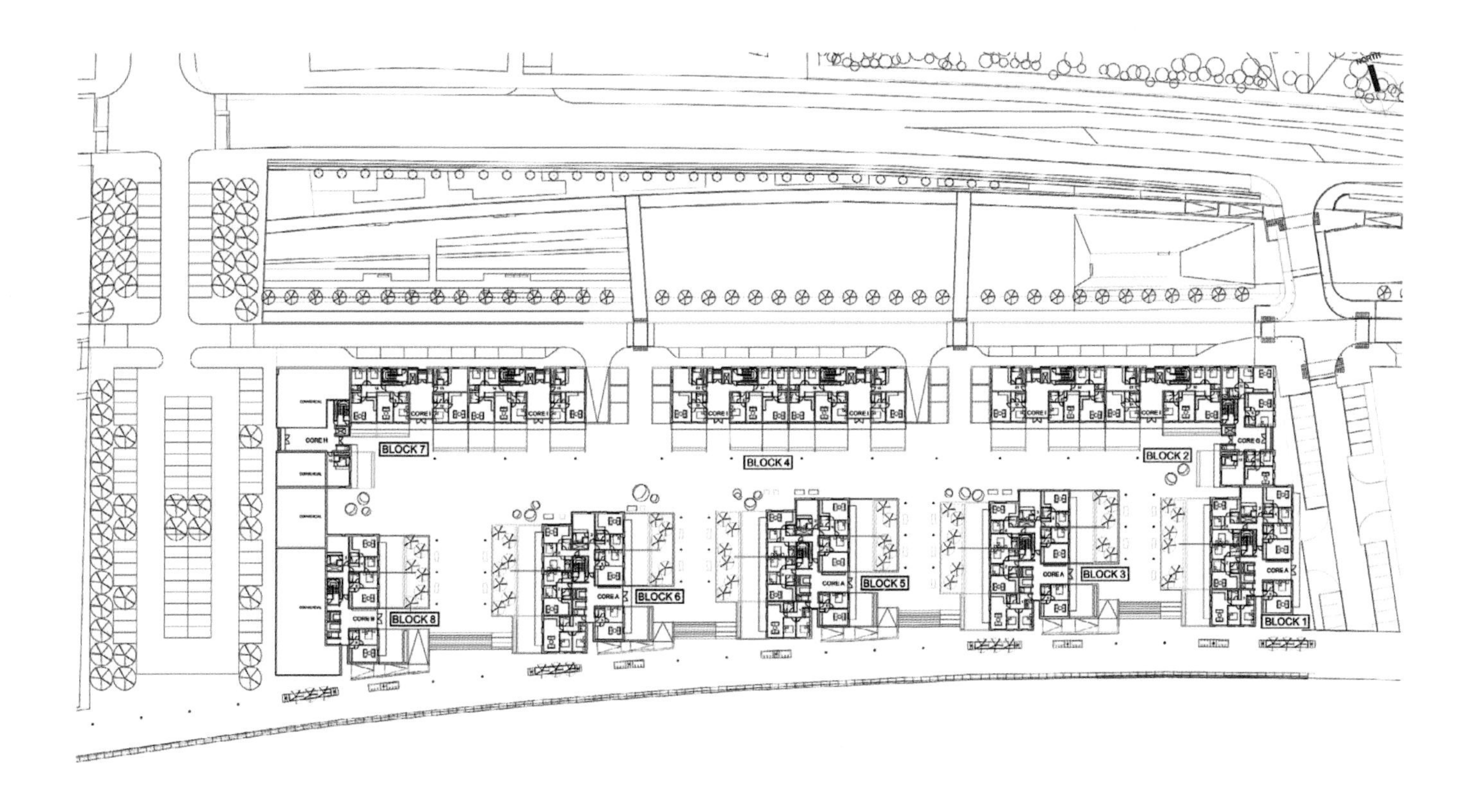

The plan for Glasgow Harbour consists of five simple towers in front of three terraces. Internal flat plans are organised to give the maximum number of occupants a view of the Clyde.

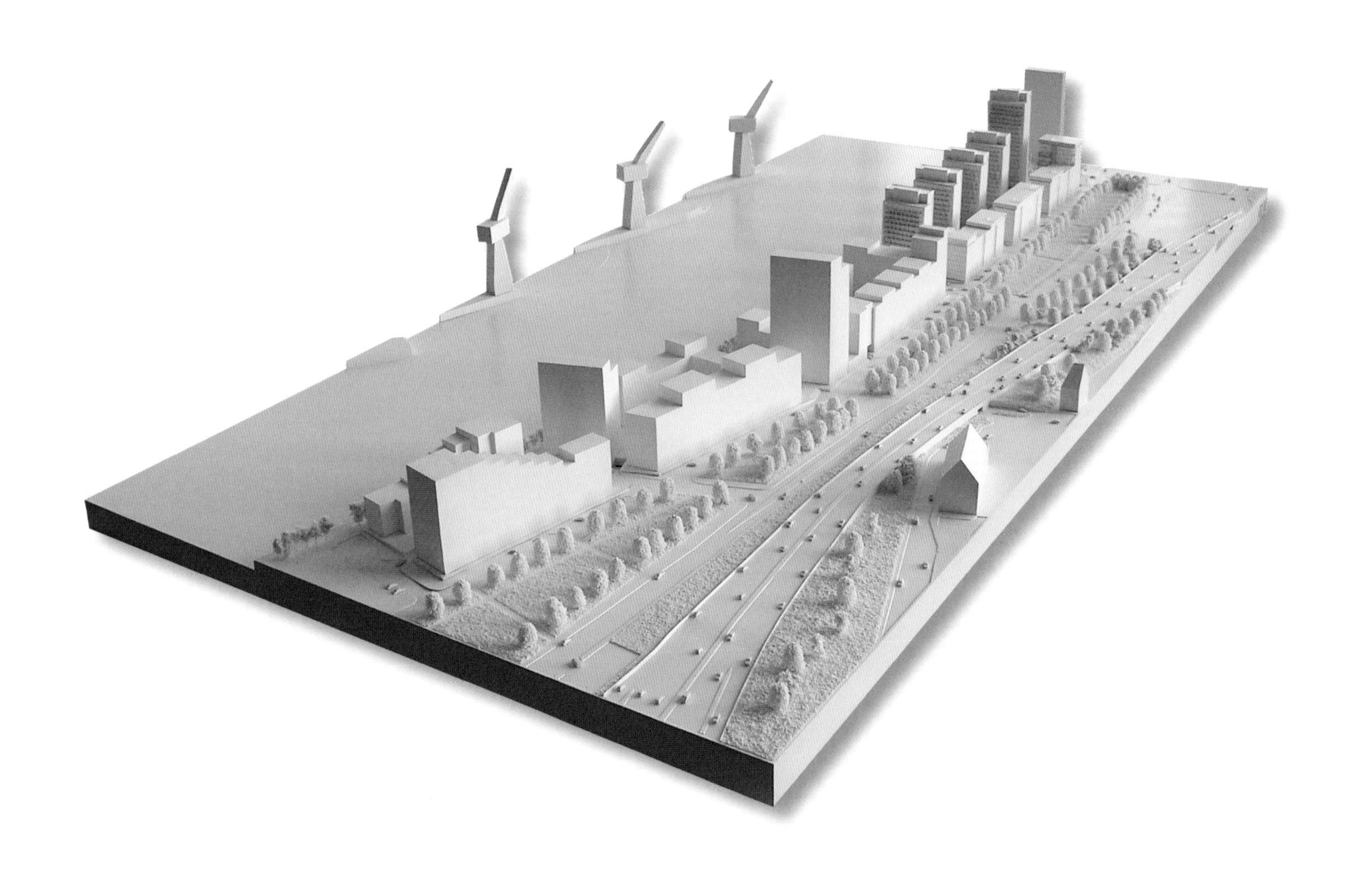

"I really agree with Rafael Moneo when he talked about the grid and then the idea of making a commentary on the grid. It's like a hand of poker, you can't go back, you never go back to the beginning again, you have to move forward." Gordon Murray

Model showing Phase 1 and Phase 2 of Glasgow Harbour.

The 14-storey towers arranged on a north-south axis on the edge of the Clyde.

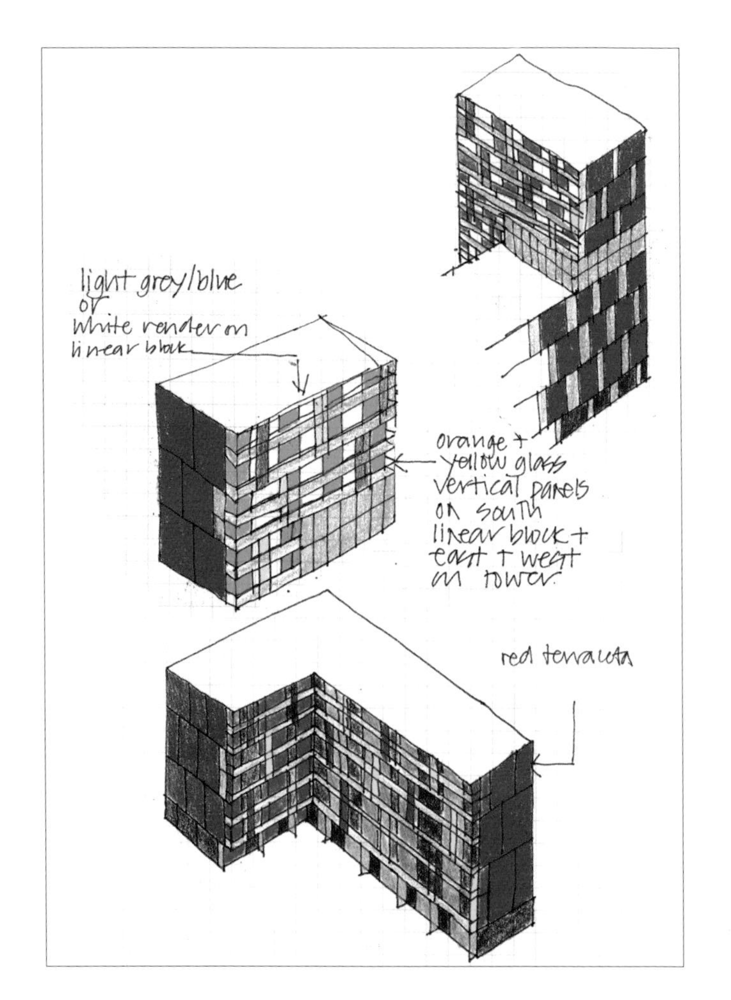

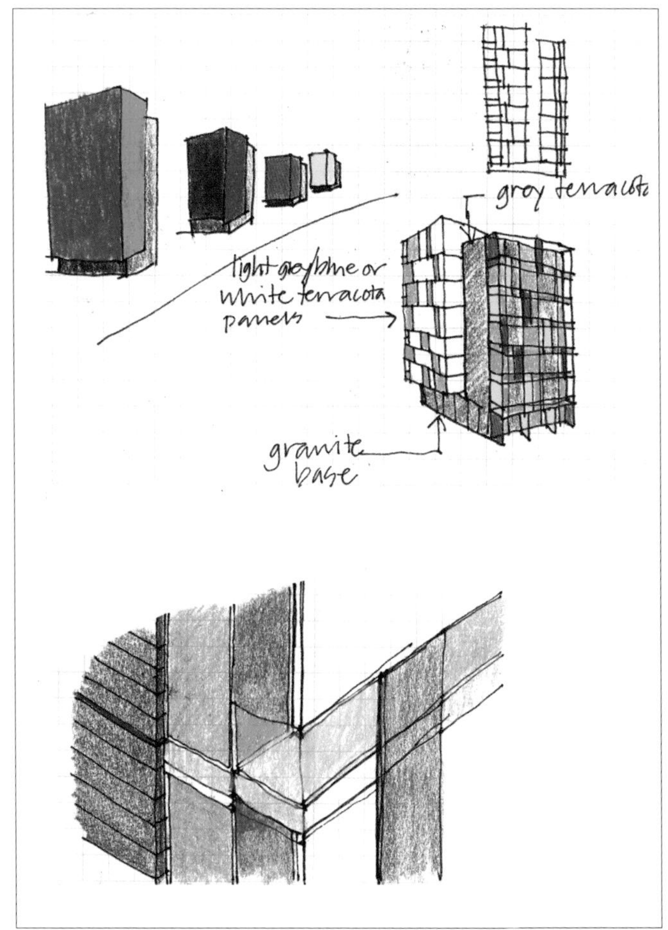

The practice spends a lot of time looking at how elevations work. These sketches are part of the study into the materials and articulation of the façades.

Research into how different cladding materials are dealt with at key junctions.

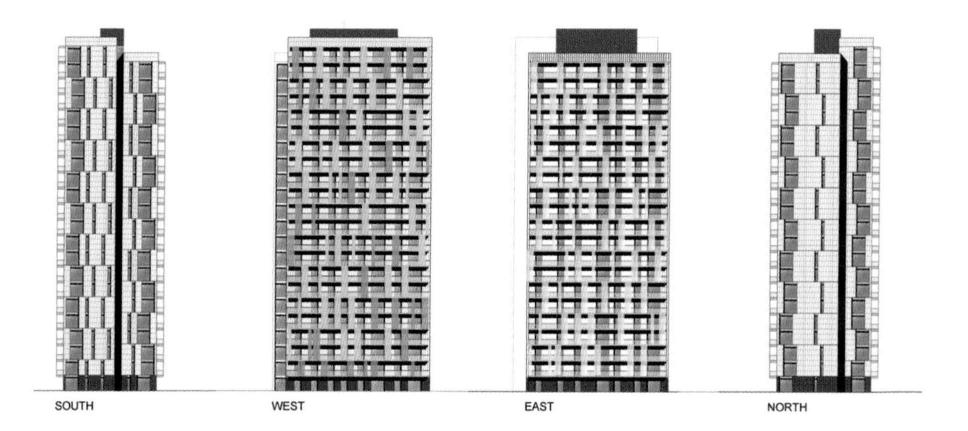

TYPICAL WEST ELEVATION: COLOUR VARIATIONS

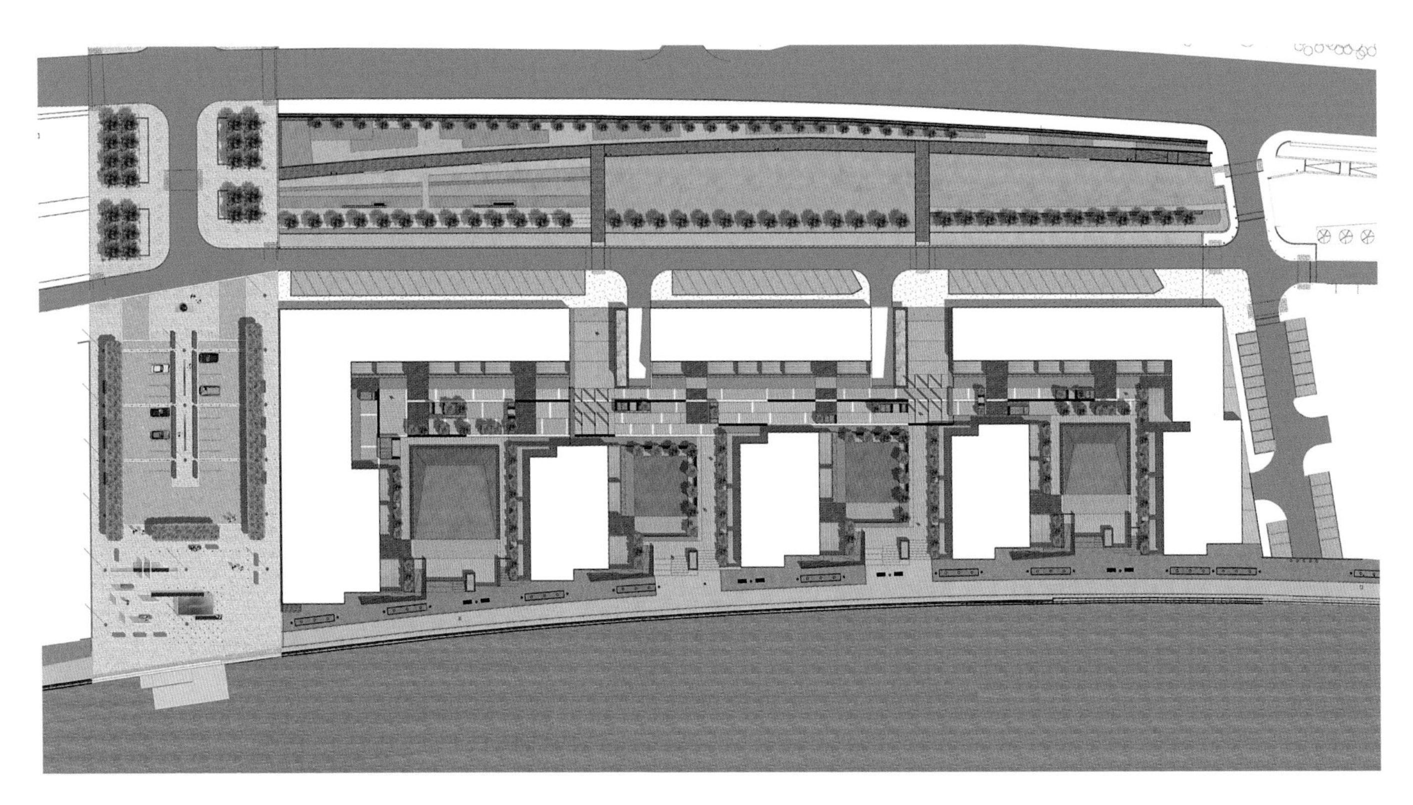

The public spaces between the proposed towers were a key concern for gm+ad. The practice has produced a structured framework for landscaping that articulates the routes around the towers and provides meaningful public spaces.

"There are people that say that cities like Glasgow are shrinking and we should build low-density accommodation that matches that shift. I think that it is important that we structure our economy and create the right mechanics to ensure that population does increase." Gordon Murray

recent works

Sentinel Building

Glasgow

SENTINEL is a £10 million, ten-storey office block built for Kenmore Property, just around the corner from the practice's earlier work, the Spectrum Building. It sits on a corner site where the city drops down towards the Clyde to the south and the grid begins to erode towards the west. It's on the very edge of the area that the city has identified as its 'financial district' and, as a result, functions as one gateway to that area. At night-time the financial core becomes the city's red-light district, so it seems somehow appropriate that the defining image of the building is the one featured on the front of this book, of Sentinel lit up with a deep rich red. The drama of the red light contained within a very refined and flush glass box epitomises the practice's best work, work that is both controlled and exciting.

The building sits close to the 1960s Anderston Centre, the mega-structure designed by Richard Seifert, with its decorative concrete and towers. gm+ad's response has a directness to match Seifert's; both buildings demonstrate what happens when you have architects that sufficiently build with a limited palette of materials and a bold form. The lobby of Sentinel provokes associations with the best of American modernism at its most generous and the robust but slightly glamorous commercial buildings produced in Edinburgh in the 1960s, such as the Scottish Provident in St Andrew Square.

The building was designed like a hinge, to form a strong edge to the financial district. This hinge sits at the back of the site and the main body of the office accommodation is located in a glass box that appears to hang between the two sides of the hinge, springing apparently unsupported from the core. The thinking behind the design is highly legible, with a degree of interest and complexity that is not usually evident in spec office buildings.

The client was looking for a column free space, so one of the drivers behind the design was the need to create an open floor plate. Structurally it proved financial impossible to cantilever the entire box; at ground level a single column supported the structure but the design of the lobby area, which is simple and enclosed with frameless glass, creates the effect of a cantilever.

The use of colour LEDs in this building has given the building a certain dramatic presence in the city that it would not have acquired otherwise. On some nights the red colour change that runs vertically from top to bottom creates the impression that the building is running with blood. When gm+ad first looked at the treatment for Sentinel it explored many options, including coloured glass panels, but in the end it opted for coloured light. The final design solution, which was developed with service engineers KJ Tait, provides a very dramatic wash of colour. The colour appears to fill the entire building rather than just lighting the edges. This effect was achieved by placing 1,200 and 600mm-long strips of LED lights around the building perimeter. The LEDs work in

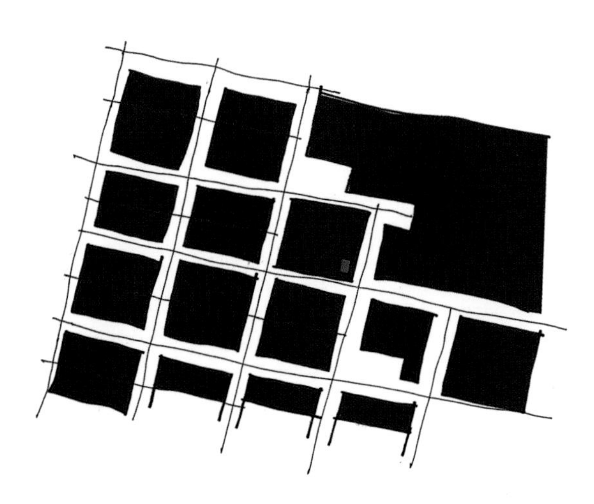

RGB mode, which allows them to create a spectrum of colours. There are two drivers on each floor to change the colour (one for the west and one for the north façade) that allows the occupiers to change the colour on each floor and on each façade independently. The system can be set to change colour in a variety of different ways.

When the ten-storey building was submitted for planning it was considered too tall by the RFACS. Since then the planning environment has changed – Elphinstone is currently working on a 30-storey tower just around the corner at Charing Cross.

Like all good Glasgow offices the Sentinel Building takes inspiration from a range of international sources. gm+ad has learned from the best of American modernism how to deal with a commercial building when it meets the ground. A good lobby needs to smell of success and have a degree of gravitas to it. It can't be like a bar, with a 'here today, gone tomorrow' dynamism, but it still needs a bit of drama. The office is also influenced by European, Dutch and German developments. The reception is red and full-blooded. Credit is due to the young architects that ran the project, Reiner Novak, the project architect, and Isabel Garriga, for the adventurous use of colour.

The client, Kenmore, is a Scottish-based investment company that usually invests in other people's buildings but wanted, on this occasion, to build its own commercial project. On most speculative office projects the agents rule the roost and demand that new buildings have a conservative exterior on the basis that a distinctive building is likely to turn off some potential tenants. In this case the client was not led by the agents, but by a positive desire to make an imprint on the city.

Sentinel has been designed to sit within the existing urban grain.

Internal view looking south.

External view along Douglas Street.

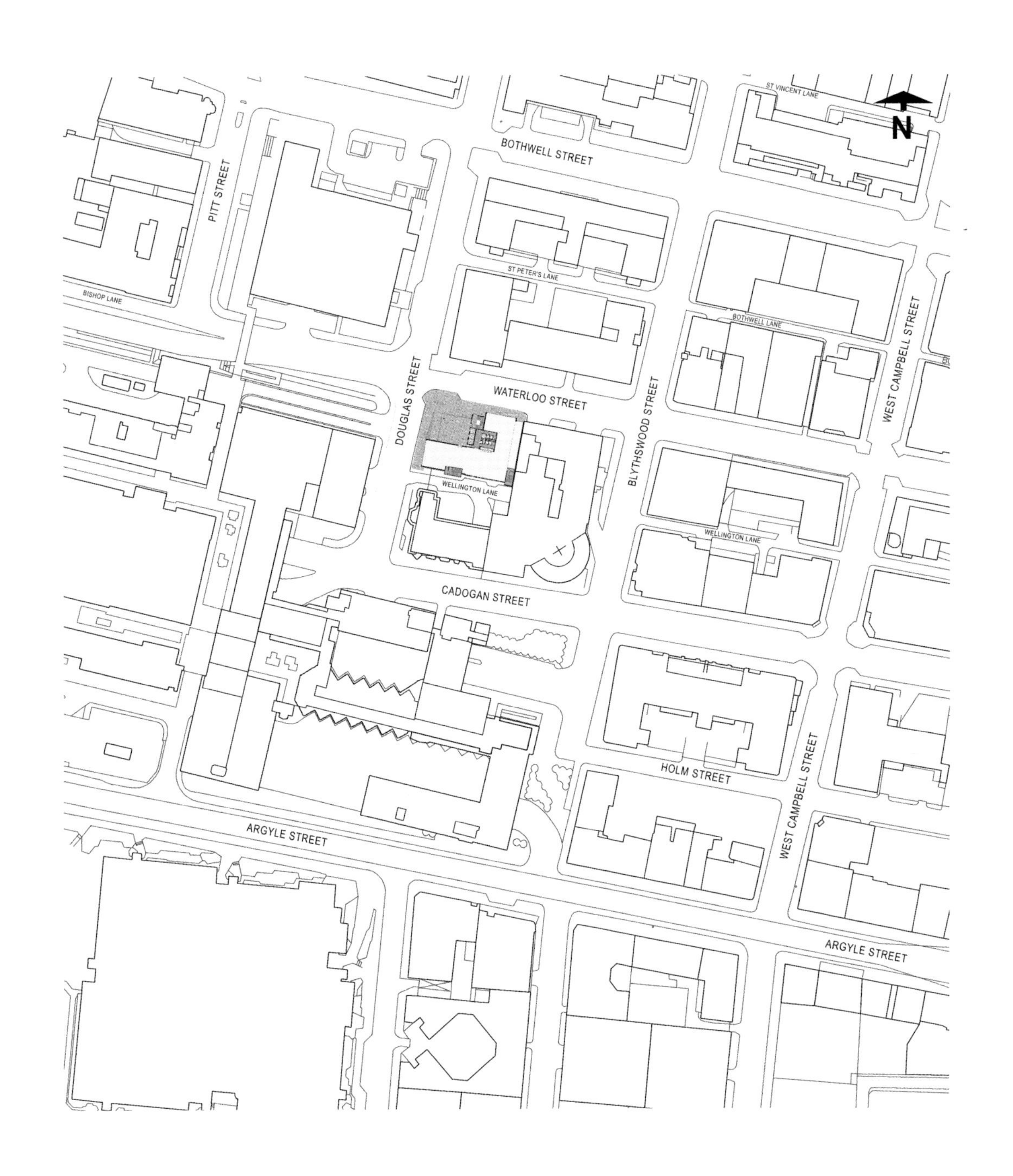

"No two buildings that we do are the same. Our architecture is based on trying to understand a problem and the people involved. There are some things that we explore in buildings that we would never do again." Gordon Murray

Site plan of Sentinel showing surrounding blocks.

Ground, first and tenth-floor plans of Sentinel. Ground floor showing relationship to the street and tenth floor showing the roof garden. The first floor demonstrates the uninterrupted quality of the interior space.

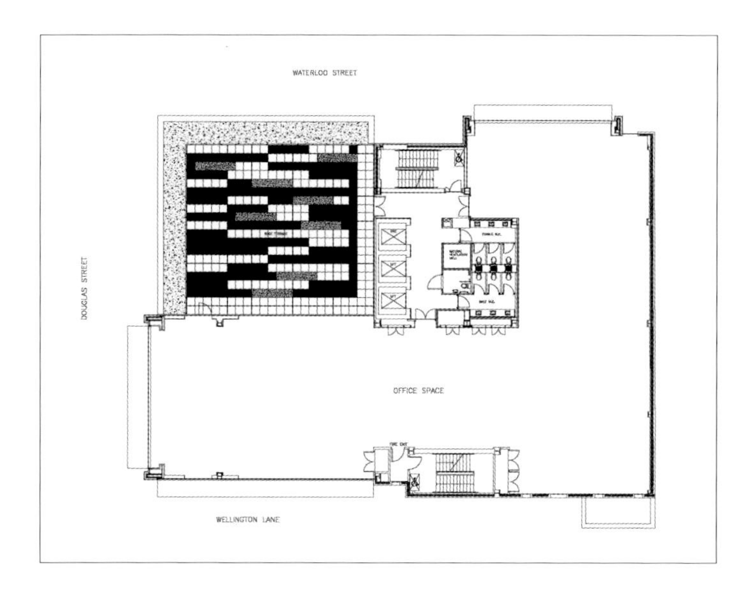

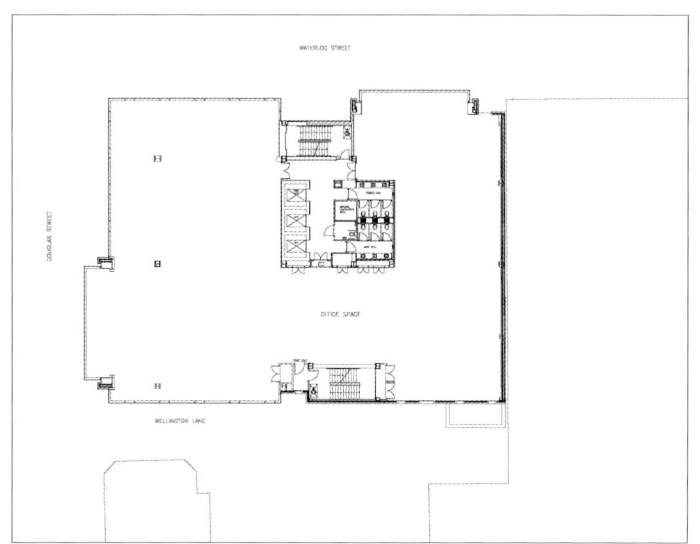

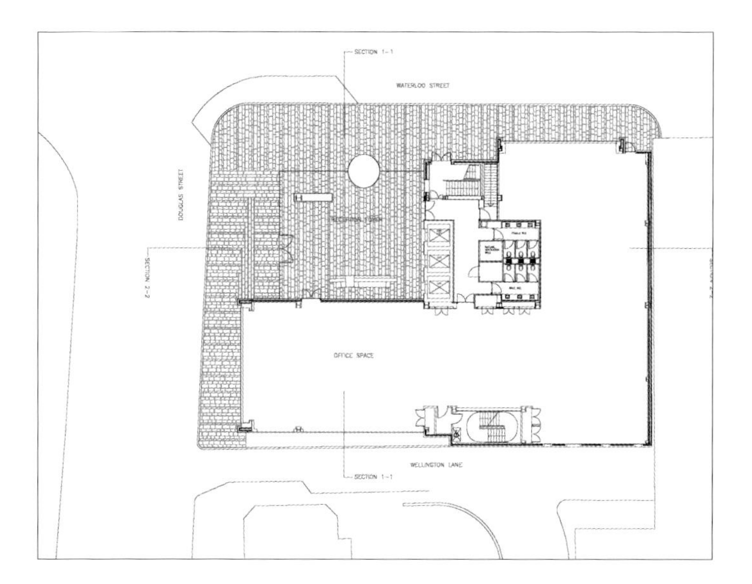

View of Sentinel looking down Waterloo Street. The rear court of the building.

The rear of the building as seen from an adjacent block.

Panorama of the city looking west from inside the office space.

"We like to think that all of our buildings are restrained. To argue that something is not restrained implies that you don't have control. Anyway restrained is not quite the right way to describe Sentinel. For a speculative office building it has an immense amount of attitude." Gordon Murray

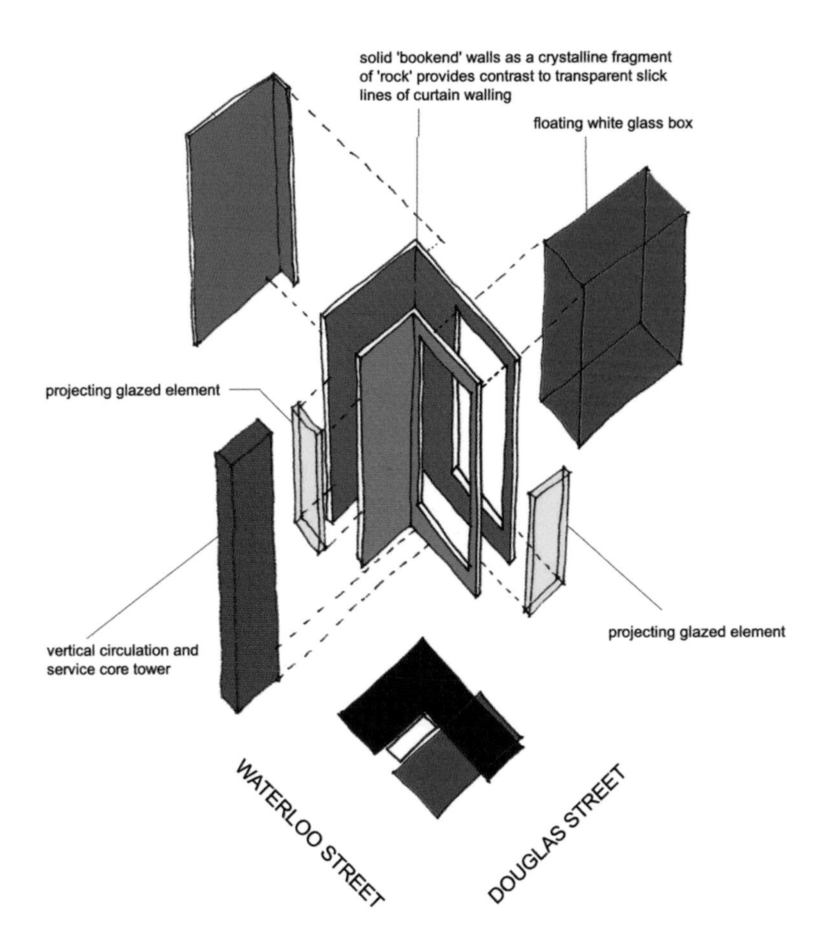

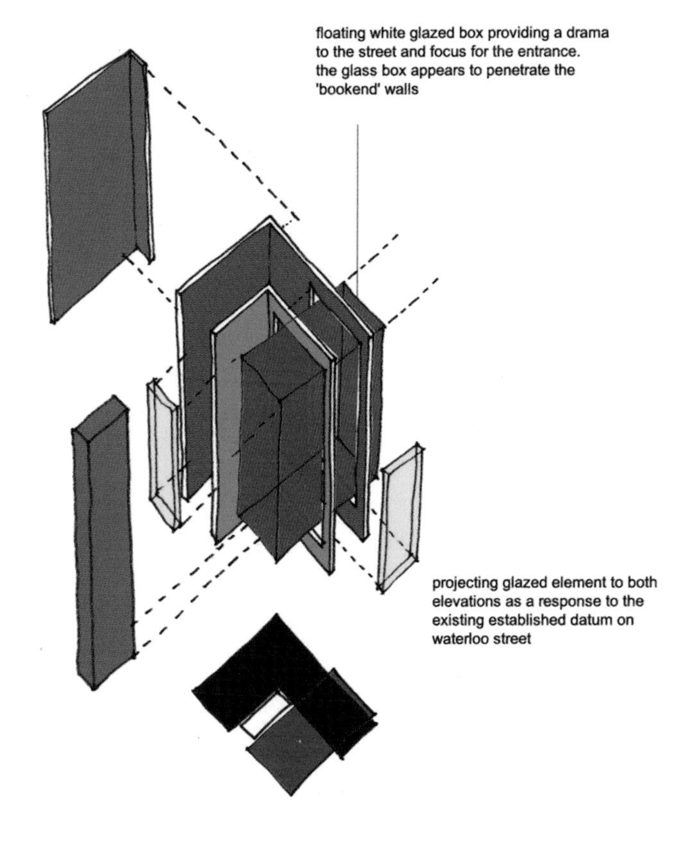

Night and day — sketches showing the building in context.

A diagram showing the concept behind the design and the basic components of the form.

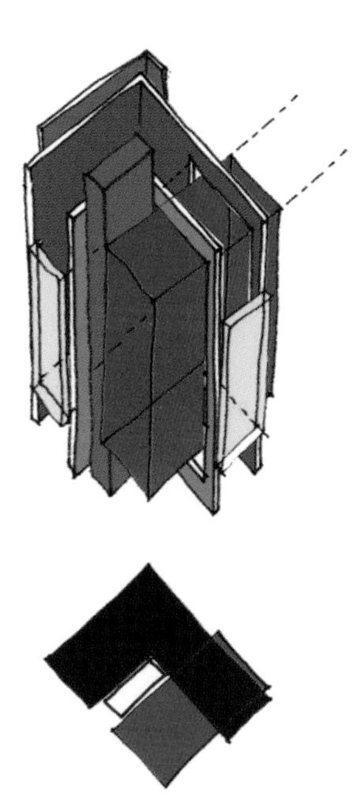

Photographs of the building at night showing the colour cycle, blue and red phases.

Sentinel
WATERLOO STREET
Sentinel

Photograph showing structural glazing.

A long section through the building's façade.

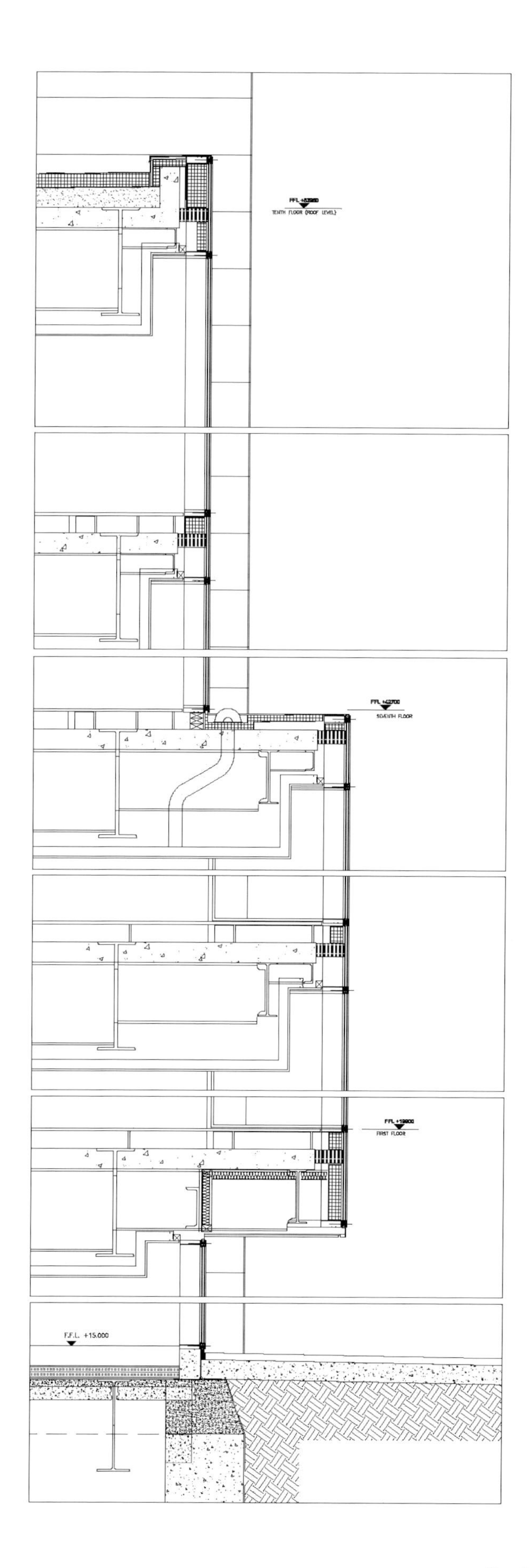

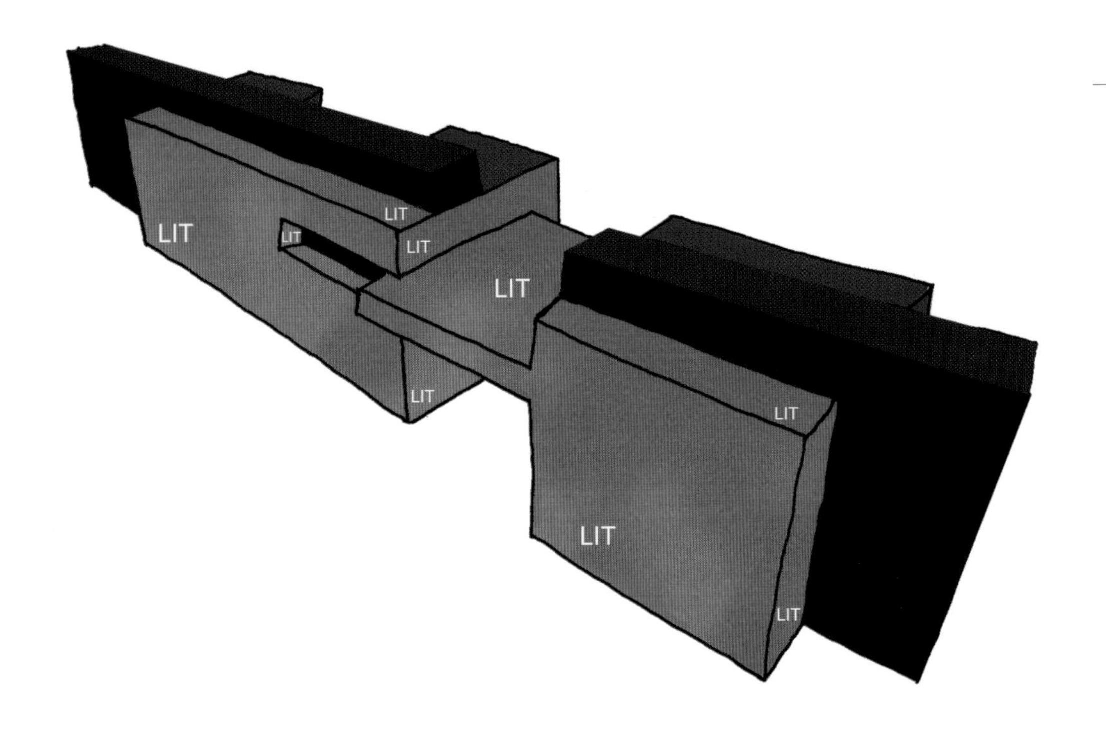

Sketches showing the design of the reception desk.

Photographs of the entrance and reception area with its frameless glass screen and Welsh slate back wall.

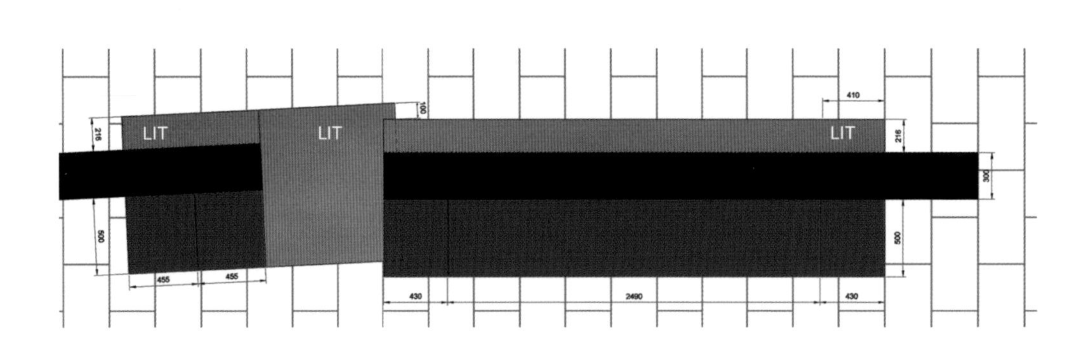

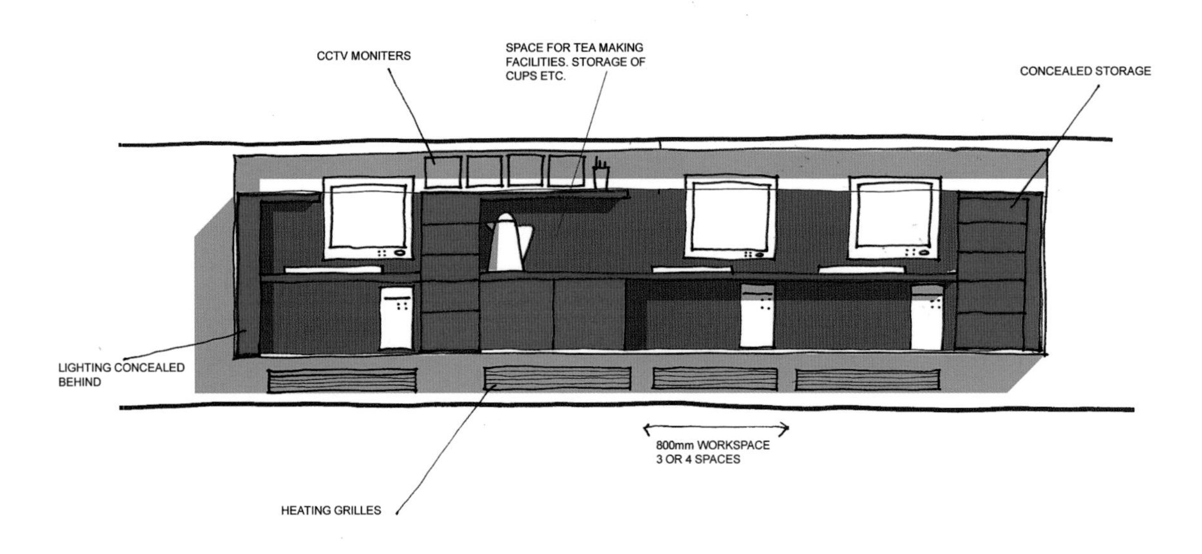

Sentinel

Sentinel

John Knox Street business units

Clydebank

THIS £1.5 million project was commissioned in May 2004 and completed just over a year later. Clydebank Re-built, and its director Eleanor McAllister, the client for John Knox Street, places a premium on design quality. It has some very good architects working for it: David Page has designed the master plan; JM Architects' Glasgow office is designing the hard landscape; and Chris Stewart Architects is refurbishing the last remaining crane on the site of the old John Brown shipyards. When gm+ad was asked to design a group of industrial starter units it wanted to do something that would in some way relate to the industrial heritage of the area, but wanted to avoid using the well-publicised association with shipbuilding.

Clydebank Re-built is one of three Urban Regeneration Companies (URC) in Scotland. It was looking for inexpensive business start-up units with a design edge. The site on John Knox Street, which is less than a hectare, was owned by West Dunbartonshire Council. It was identified for the first stage of development and a funding package assembled for West Dunbartonshire Council and Strathclyde European Partnership money from the ERDF. The site sits on the main road into Clydebank, so it was important that Clydebank Re-built had some visual presence, for its own marketing needs, but also as part of the broader regeneration of the area.

The brief was straightforward and the budget tight, so the architects undertook a number of exercises in arranging simple building blocks on the site and settled for a square of blocks enclosing a central court, or 'defensible space'. The blocks are pretty basic internally; those on the corners have a mezzanine floor that occupies the lantern spaces, which are expressed externally through the polycarbonate glazing. At the same time the practice was working with colour and light at Sentinel, so it used this experience on the Clydebank project.

gm+ad wanted to use the cladding to give the building a distinct identity. The practice looked at the way in which contemporary Dutch designers use materials in original and quirky ways and, after exploring a wide range of different materials, they settled for coloured Eternit panels with pattern transfers.

The pattern, known as Castle stitch, was one of the stitches found on Singer sewing machines. Singer was one of the largest employers in Clydebank until it closed its factory in 1980. Writing about the scheme in the *Architect's Journal*, Neil Gillespie said: "The workshops explore this fascination with the fetish of surface. These most basic of building types display an intelligence and enquiry that is palpable. The massing is elegant, the cladding is tailored and well cut."

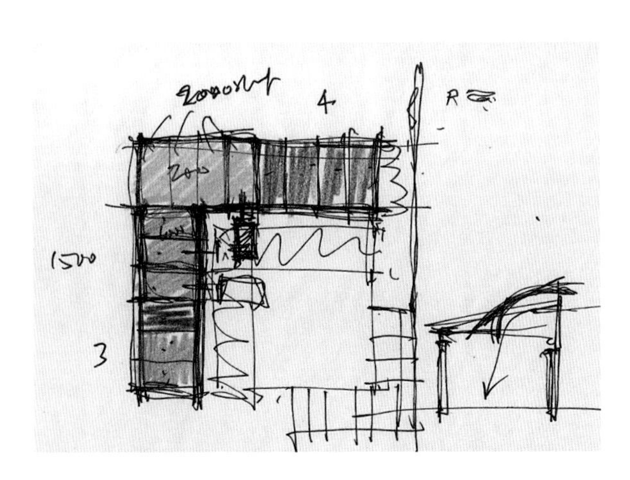

Roadside view of a single unit showing cladding and the building's polycarbonate light box.

Detailed shot of cladding and light box.

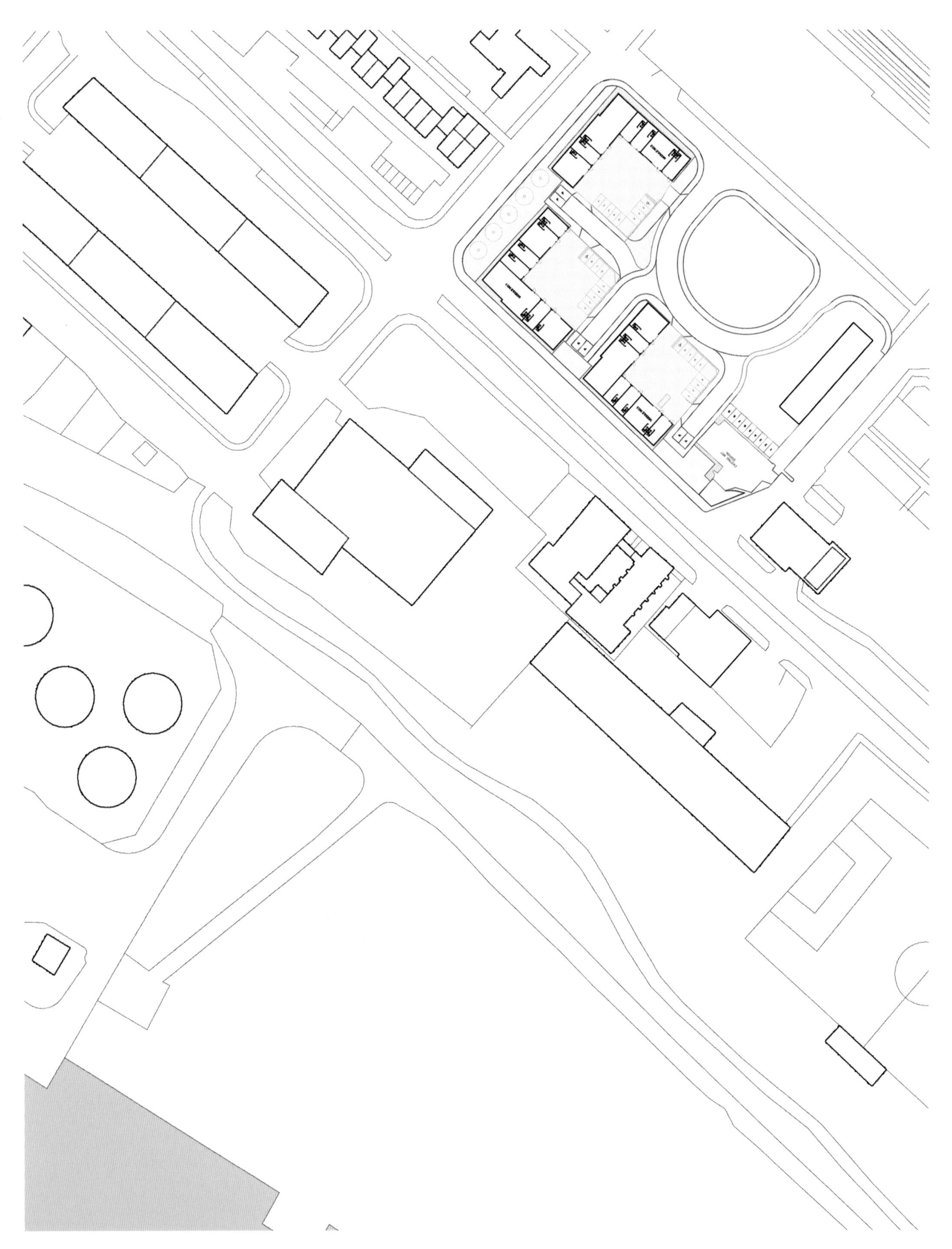

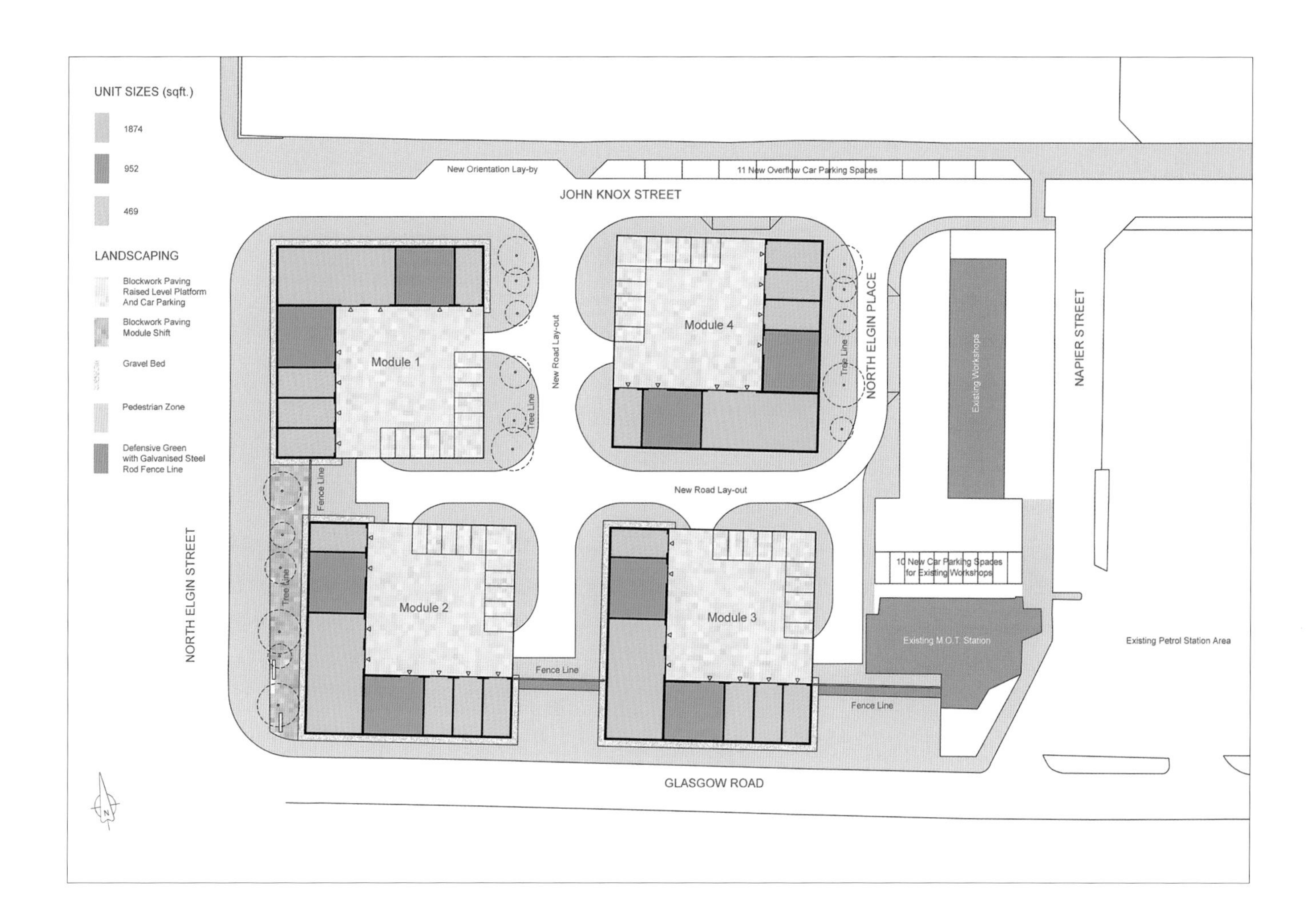

Plan showing the John Knox site in context.

The site plan showing four L-shaped units organised around courts.

The workshops with views of the Kilpatrick Hills behind.

A study in colour and elevation treatment.

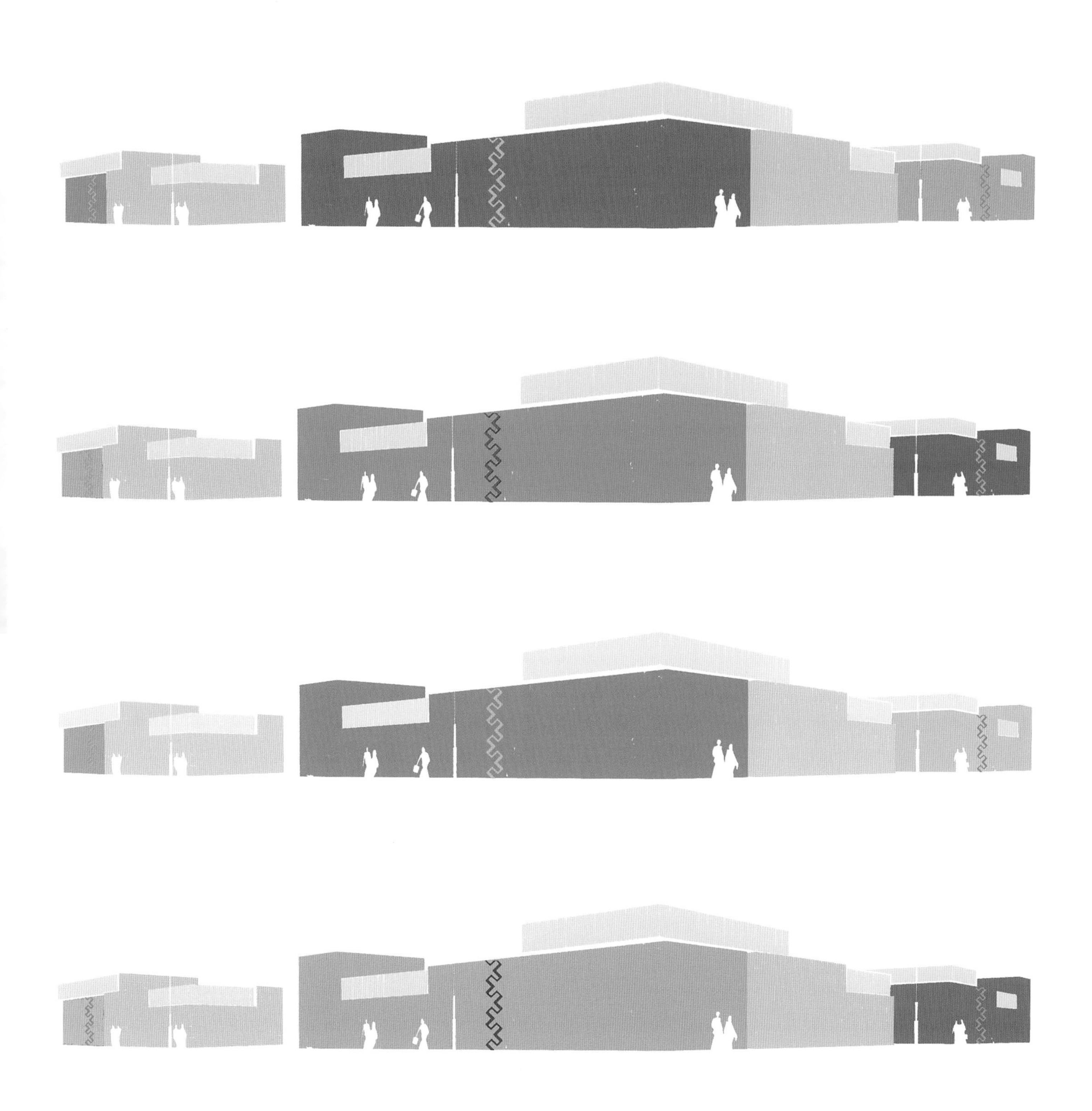

'The Castle' stitching pattern, taken from Singers standard stitches, has been reproduced to decorate the cladding panels.

A drawing by 'Greek' Thomson demonstrating the relationship between surface and decoration.

Elevations showing cladding panel decoration.

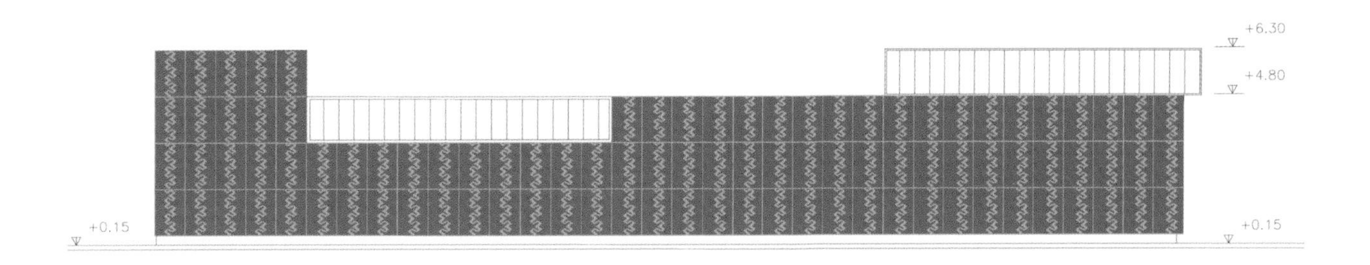
+6.30
+4.80
+0.15
+0.15

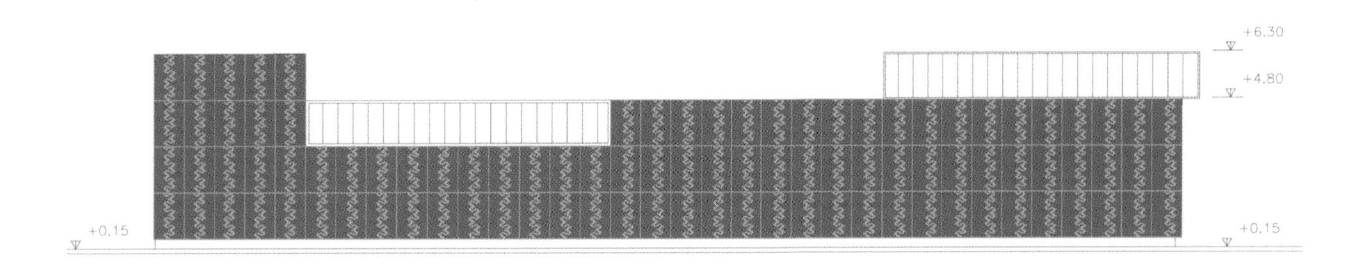
+6.30
+4.80
+0.15
+0.15

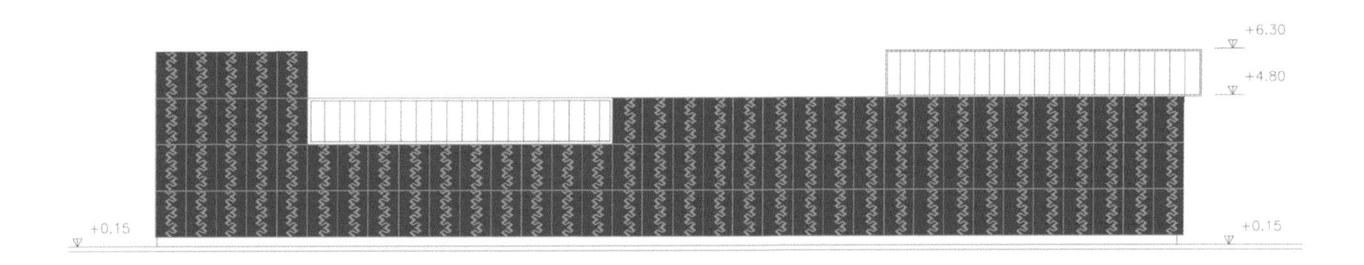
+6.30
+4.80
+0.15
+0.15

River Heights

Glasgow

THE Broomielaw runs west along the north bank of the Clyde from Glasgow's city centre. It is a former industrial area previously occupied by warehouses, now the subject of piecemeal developments for the commercial and residential sector. River Heights is located close to the point where the Kingston Bridge sweeps over the river road. The residential block for FM developments consists of 102 flats providing a range of accommodation from two-bedroom flats to penthouses. In addition there is a retail unit at ground level and parking at basement and ground levels.

Although the site overlooks the Clyde, a low-rise development built during the 1980s occupies the land across the road and immediately opposite the river so the architects decided to place all of the flats on the second floor upwards to ensure that all of the units benefited from the close relationship to the river.

At 13 storeys, the scale of River Heights reflects the commercial needs of the client, but it also feels appropriate. Scale is difficult in such environments; buildings need to be robust enough to sit alongside the remaining titanic old red-brick warehouses at the same time as engendering a major leap in the manner in which they meet the ground and respond to the new users, which are no longer dock workers and freight vehicles, but home-owners.

This £10 million project is really an exercise in scale and represents one of the few serious attempts to generate activity at road level on the stretch. The palette of materials has been carefully chosen, not to reflect the latest specification fad (white render and timber) but to create something that works with the general grain and texture of this part of the city. A black, granite-clad podium with a generous and formal street entrance, containing a commercial unit and access to parking, is the first attempt on this part of the street to grapple with the difficult task of creating activity on the road at the same time as engaging with the giant scale of the surrounding buildings.

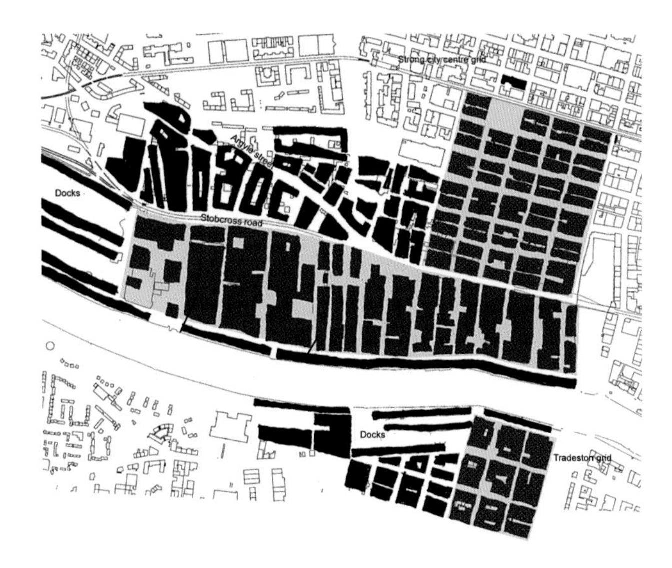

LANCEFIELD STREET
HYDEPARK STREET
WARROCH STREET
CHEAPSIDE STREET
LANCEFIELD QUAY
ANDERSTON QUAY
RIVER CLYDE
LOWER HARBOUR

A site plan of River Heights showing the relationship between the building and the Clyde.

Floor plans of the building. Ground floor with space for parking, a retail unit and the lobby. Second-floor plan showing shared external spaces and upper-floor plan showing flat layouts.

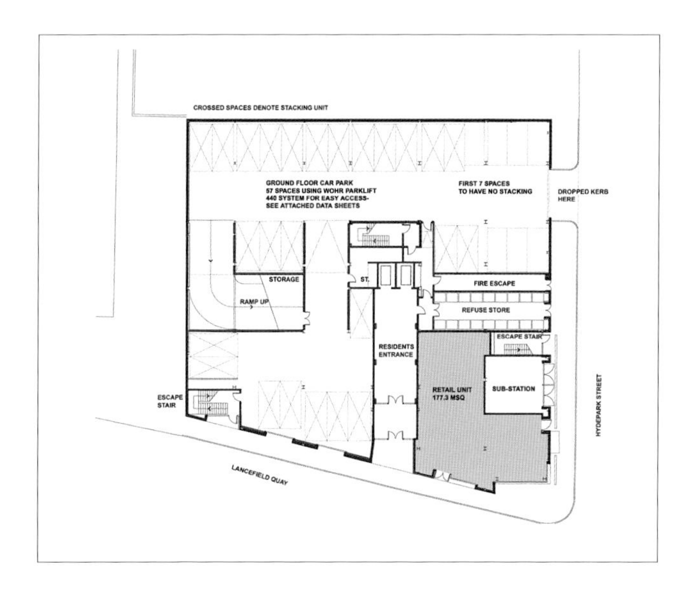

Photographs showing the building from the south side of the Clyde.

A model showing the building mass.

Early sketches showing the relationship between the building, surrounding buildings and the river.

Shared external space on the building's roof. The stone cladding at street level arranged in bands of polished and flamed granite.

A detail of the screening to the east elevation of the block. The entrance to the shared lobby finished with zinc.

RIVER HEIGHTS

Radisson SAS Hotel

Glasgow

IN 1998 gm+ad won an invited competition to design a five-star hotel on the west side of Argyle Street. Shortly after the competition Marylebone Warwick and Balfour acquired the site and retained gm+ad to develop the scheme. Radisson SAS was contracted as operator and the brief was fixed on a four-star 250-bedroom hotel. Work began on site in September 1999 and was completed in 2002.

Argyle Street runs east-west through the heart of Glasgow cutting under Central Station. The new Radisson SAS sits behind the station in an area earmarked as part of the city's new financial district. However, most of the new developments within the financial district have taken place on the riverfront and Argyle Street remains run down, populated by budget hotels, shabby tenements and uninspiring shops.

The hotel's design is a very interesting response to an uninspiring context. The dominant feature is a massive copper-clad screen that forms one side of a full-height atrium. The 60-metre-long screen, punctuated by a simple cantilevered slate-clad black box, is supported on seven fluted pilotti and appears to stand independently of the rest of the building. At ground level the atrium is fully glazed and houses a number of public functions. The decision to produce such a simple blank façade onto Argyle Street generated criticism during construction but over time it has been recognised as a good example of how to deal with the grid and the scale of an evolving but largely Victorian city centre.

The design has succeeded in bringing a touch of glamour and drama to a building type that had, in Scotland's major cities, been squeezed of any sense of romance or vitality. The Radisson evokes parallels with some of the USA's best hotels on its grandest streets. Glass lifts glide up and down the five-storey atrium while the black slate-clad box punches its way through the copper façade. Guests cross a glass bridge over the atrium to the suite of specialist rooms contained within the box.

As a result of the facade treatment there is a very strong relationship between activity on the street and that inside the atrium; it's a genuine inside-outside space where residents can watch the world go by, a difficult thing to achieve in such a tight urban environment. The planning of the hotel is as simple and clear as the concept of the copper screen. The rooms are organised in a u-shape overlooking a south-facing central court, beneath which sits the hotel's banqueting room. On the west side of the building a number of the hotel rooms are contained within a B-listed baroque building which is seamlessly incorporated into the new building.

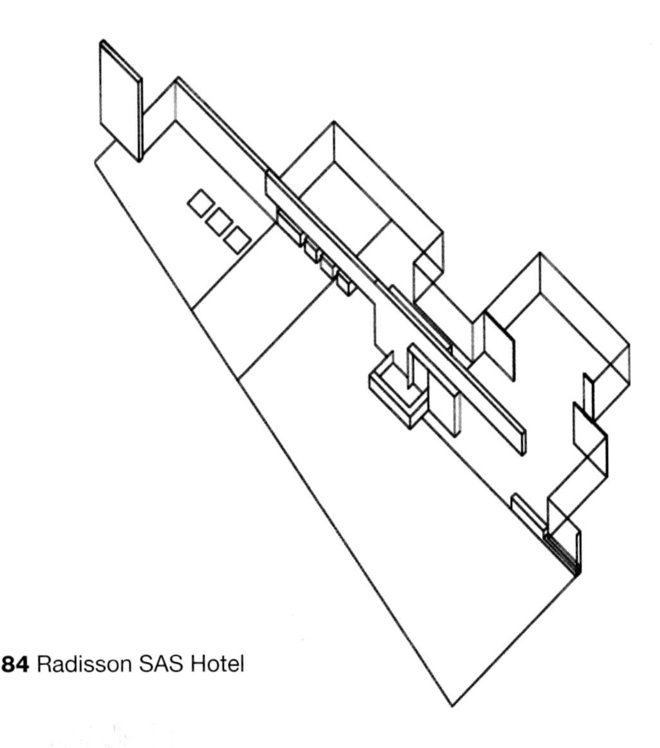

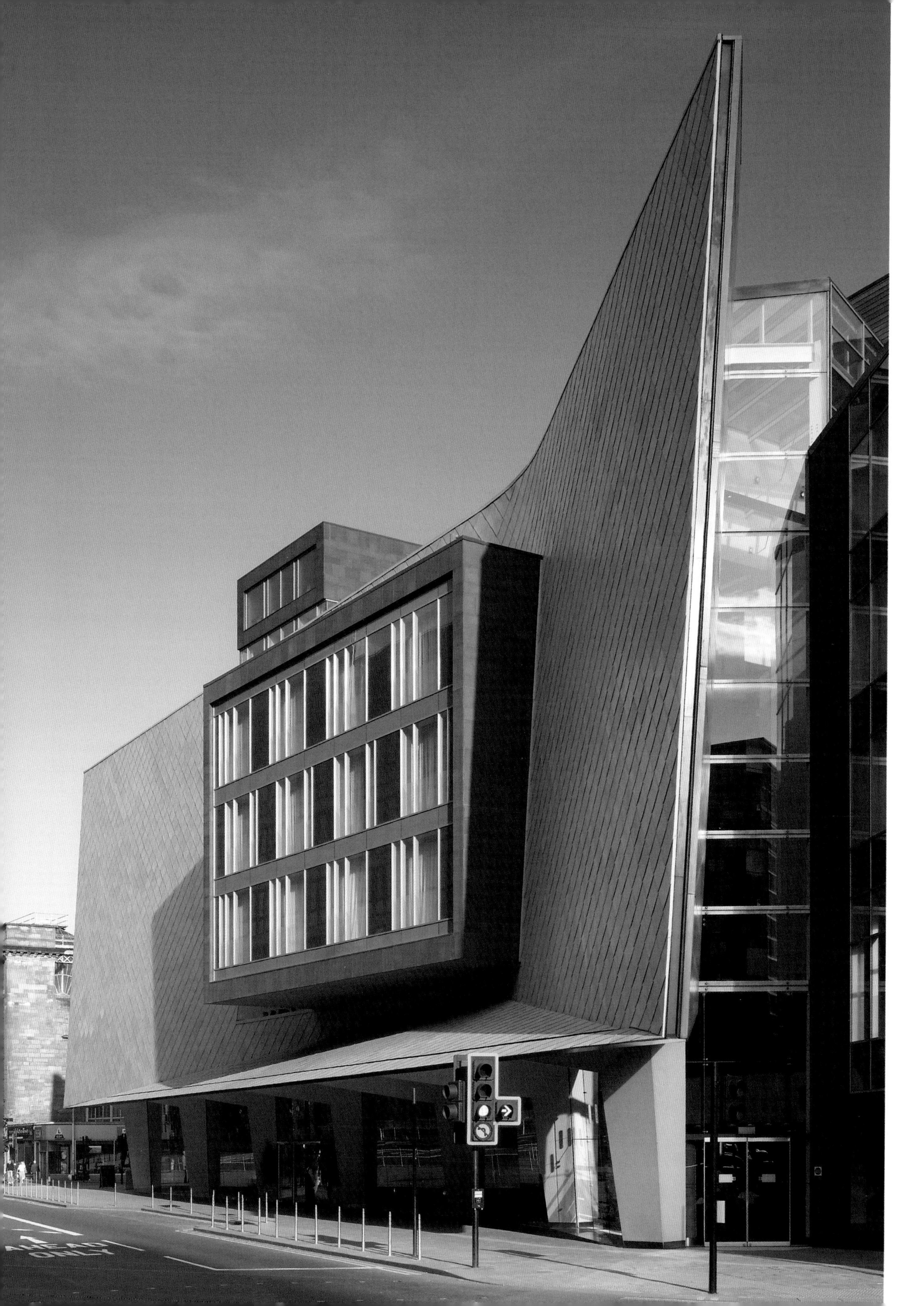
AHEAD ONLY

Full metal jacket

By Jonathan Glancey

GLASGOW, copper; copper, Glasgow. Here are a city and a material made for one another. Think of the steamships built, from 1811, at Partick and Govan on the Clyde. Remember the locomotives built, from 1862, by Neilsen Reid, and from 1903 by the North British works at Springburn. Recall such characterful buildings as Glasgow Cathedral and the Church of Our Lady of Good Counsel in Dennistoun, built in 1964-66 by those unrepentant Glaswegian modernisers, Gillespie Kidd and Coia. All made extensive use of the dull orange metal that turns magically green when exposed to air.

Now, Glaswegian architects Gordon Murray and Alan Dunlop have inserted a vast, prow-like sheet of copper into the very heart of the city. This eye-catching sheet forms the Argyle Street façade of the new £30m, 247-bedroom Radisson SAS Hotel, a block away from Glasgow Central station. It is dramatic to say the least, especially at night, when the great copper wall, punched through with a three-storey cluster of rooms projecting over the pavement below, catches and reflects the lights of the city. And when rain falls, the copper sheens, adding to the building's lustre.

"There is a tendency to expect architects to use sandstone, sandstone and, erm, sandstone in the design and construction of new buildings in the city," says Alan Dunlop. "It is a bit of a cliché. We wanted to reflect Glasgow's historic use of metals. We've had local people call us and say the building's ugly and that we should have used the local red stone. But Glasgow is not Edinburgh – it's a tougher place altogether. We wanted to capture some of its robustness and vigour in a way that nodded, without being overly sentimental, to the past while looking, perhaps a little cockily, to the future."

All but stripped of heavy industries, Glasgow has turned to culture, cafes and conferences to power it into the 21st century. In 1990 it enjoyed a year as European City of Culture, and in 1999 was European City of Architecture and Design. And yet the city centre still lacks a number of the key buildings that could complete its new image. Until Murray and Dunlop's four-star Radisson SAS, one of these was a big, high-class, modern hotel.

The new building rises from a site that once housed tenements, but stood empty for 15 years. "It was always going to be a big building," says Dunlop, "so we thought of ways in which, rather than just filling up the available space on the site, we could offer something back to the street and the people using it." So the architects came up with the idea of the screen. It creates a pedestrian passage between the body of the hotel and the pavement's edge; it is also lower than the main building, giving the illusion that the hotel is no higher than existing 19th-century buildings along Argyle Street. Despite its scale and drama, the hotel is trying to be a respectful neighbour. And, within reason, its public spaces are open to anyone.

The smart interior is made of clean-lined modern surfaces and materials; the walls of the internal courtyard, meanwhile, are white and light, interspersed with panels of mahogany. The enfolding architecture is rigorous. "As a counterpoint to the flexible and lightweight screen," says Dunlop, "the main part of the hotel was designed to be solid, even monolithic, so we clad the walls in slate." The overall effect is memorably gritty and glamorous, with a real integrity of purpose and construction. Dunlop and Murray set up their practice together in 1996, but are

yet to win coveted commissions in Glasgow's booming arts and cultural sector. Although the duo's designs for social and private housing in Glasgow and a business park in Edinburgh have been inventive, purposeful and energetic, they have earned them the label 'commercial architects', best left to office blocks and hotels. But what a hotel. And what an office block they created recently on Glasgow's Blythswood Road. The Spectrum Building is distinguished by its shining steel cladding. Local people call it the 'Bacofoil Building'. It shows how the design of an office block can be something special with just a little artistry and a use of materials that are as much a part of the fabric of the city as red sandstone.

"There's a kind of snobbery these days," says Dunlop, "whereby architects who appear to specialise in one kind of building are not expected to do another. I hope that what we've been able to show is that it is possible to create a commercial architecture of some cultural worth." In fact, there is a long tradition of just this sort of architecture in Glasgow. Through the fissures of the copper screen on Argyle Street, guests at the Radisson SAS can peer out, not just to city monuments but to the Buck's Head Building (1863-8) designed by Alexander 'Greek' Thomson, the great commercial Glaswegian architect whose designs for Victorian office blocks and warehouses found inspiration in the styles of Ancient Greece and the Middle East, while taking advantage of the new metal technologies emerging in shipyards and locomotive works at the city's edge.

Along with distinguished commercial buildings, Thomson (1817-75) designed magnificent suburban villas, grand funeral monuments and two of the finest, most original European churches of his time, those at Glasgow's Caledonia Road and St Vincent Street (the latter was declared a UNESCO World Heritage Site in 2000). What his fecund career proved was that it was possible to create a cultured and innovative architecture for commerce by applying the kind of artistry normally reserved for churches and grand houses, while drawing on new technology to ensure each design would be efficient and popular among Glasgow's merchant class.

Today, the architecture of commerce and culture are all too often widely divided: little creative or visual effort appears to go into the former, while a great deal is invested in the latter. Murray and Dunlop are demonstrating that the road trod by such creative pioneers as Thomson is still very much an option. Hotels run on tight budgets by competitive chains fishing for conference trade do not need to be banal; nor do office blocks, as the Bacofoil Building proves.

The character and strength of a city like Glasgow turns on the balance between commerce and culture. Monuments, art galleries and 100 ways of serving coffee are not enough to make a city centre great. Everyday buildings need to be not just of a high standard, but truly a part of the cities they serve. And just as Thomson looked to the past to inform the present and future, so Glasgow's architects might choose to look carefully, as Murray and Dunlop have with their design for the Radisson SAS, at the city's rich heritage, which is as much to do with steel, iron and copper as with sandstone and architectural convention.

Jonathan Glancey
Previously published in The Guardian

Views along Argyle Street showing the original site prior to construction and a photograph of the new building in context.

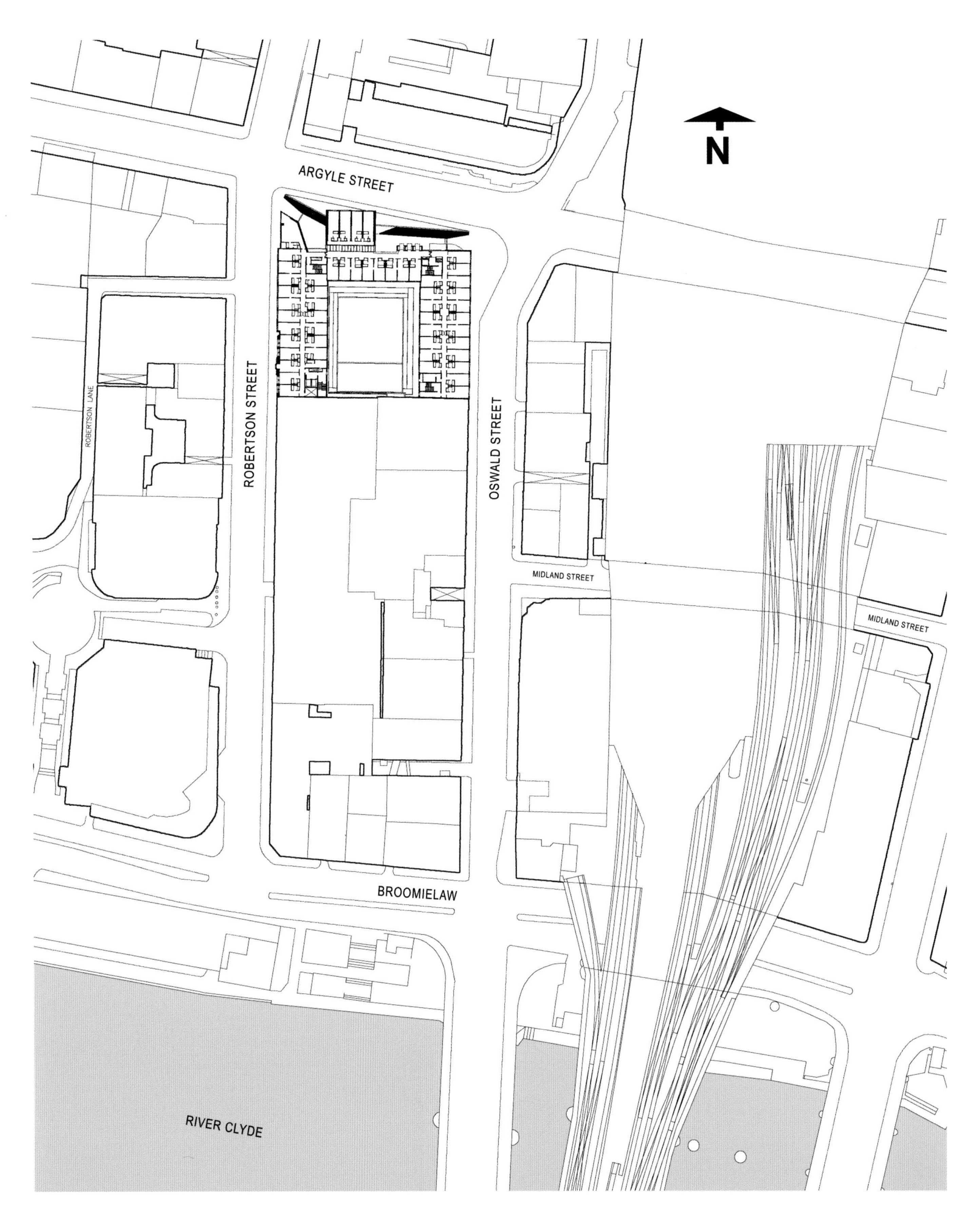
N
ARGYLE STREET
ROBERTSON STREET
ROBERTSON LANE
OSWALD STREET
MIDLAND STREET
MIDLAND STREET
BROOMIELAW
RIVER CLYDE

Area plan showing the Radisson Hotel and its relationship to Glasgow's Central station.

Site plans of the Radisson Hotel, first floor showing the conference accommodation, second floor showing the rooms and the gallery level.

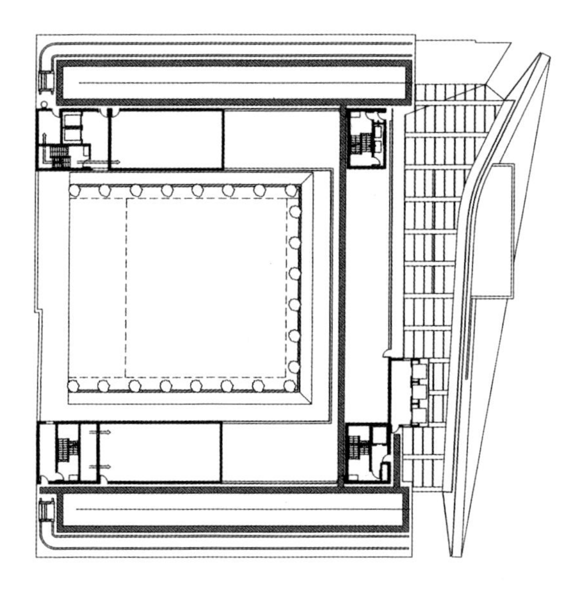

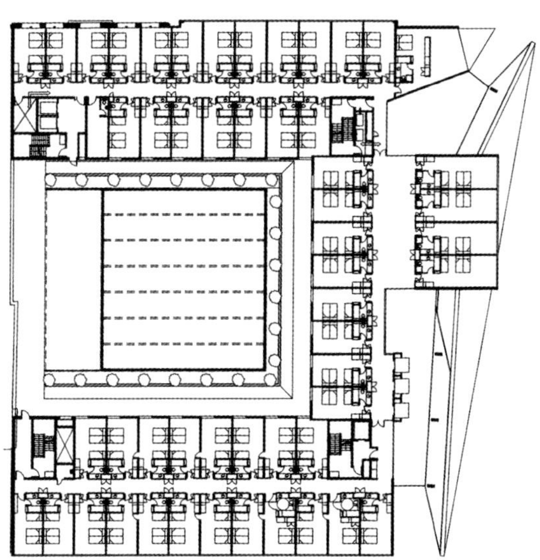

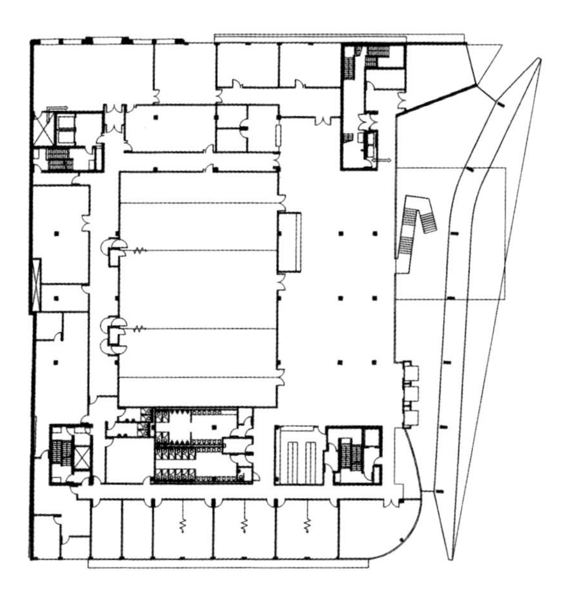

The south-facing courtyard at the Radisson has a very distinct character. In contrast to the exuberant entrance elevation, the court is a restrained, but playful exercise in dealing with the repetition of a single element associated with hotel design.

The Collage Bar is located on the eastern corner of the hotel. East elevation is heavily glazed with black slate cladding.

The interior of the lobby showing the glass bridge reaching over the lobby area to the conference accommodation.

Sketches of the west elevation and front elevation.

Photograph of the east/west façade of the Radisson which incorporates the existing B-listed building into the block.

“The most important thing to me is site and context. Our work is not contextual in the sense that it has to fit in with the surroundings. It is contextual in that it is created at a point in time.” Alan Dunlop

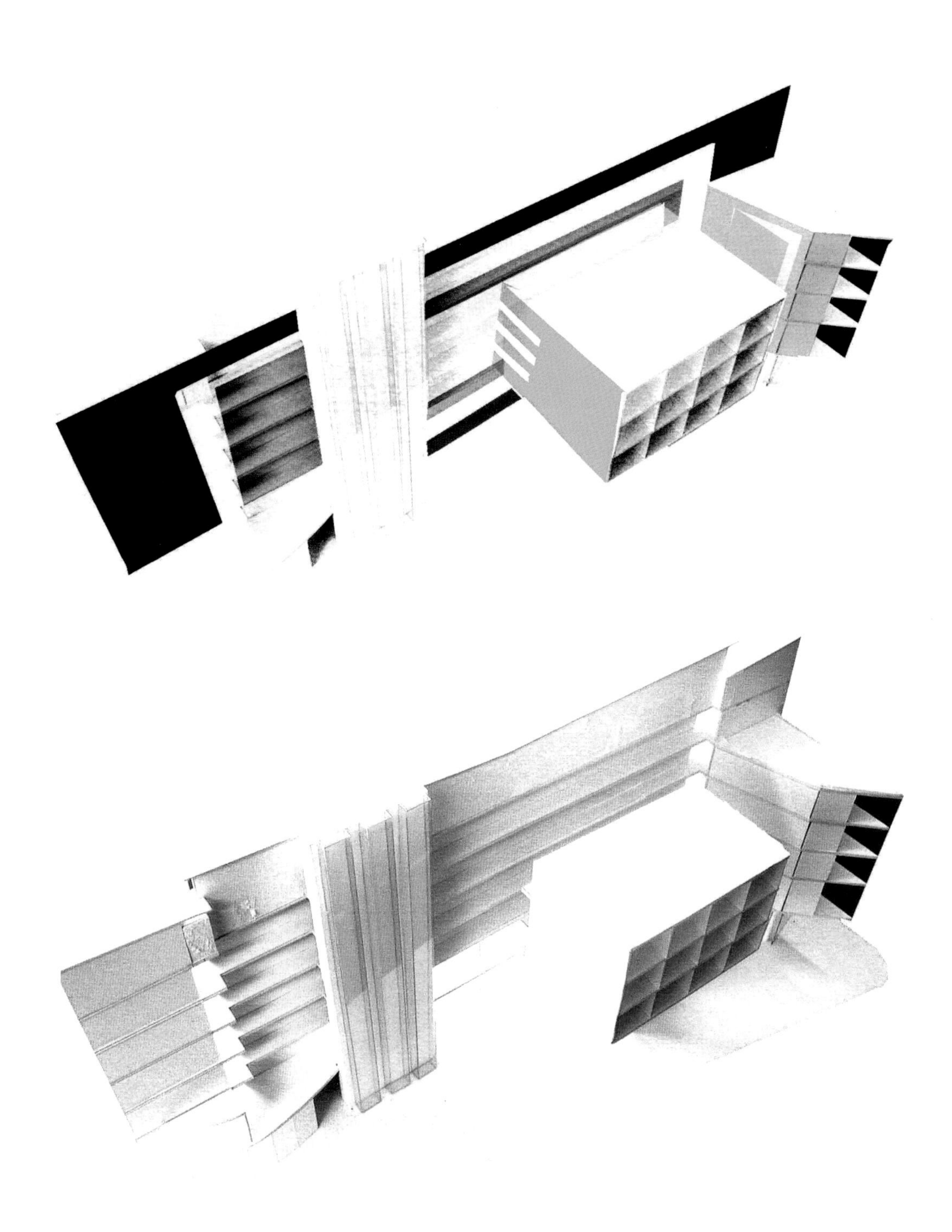

Early graphic models drawn to explore the relationship between the entrance lobby area and the box of special accommodation. Models produced to refine the design of the columns supporting the entrance canopy.

Photograph of the view along the canopy of the entrance area.

Interior shots of the lobby area. The bar and lounge and the glass screen that runs parallel to the street.

The open stair from the lobby to the conference facilities on the first floor and computer model.

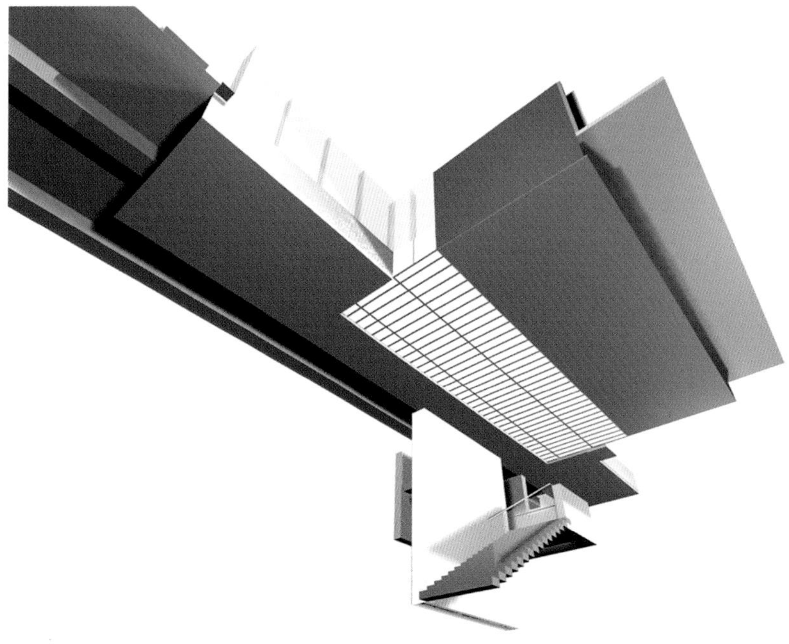

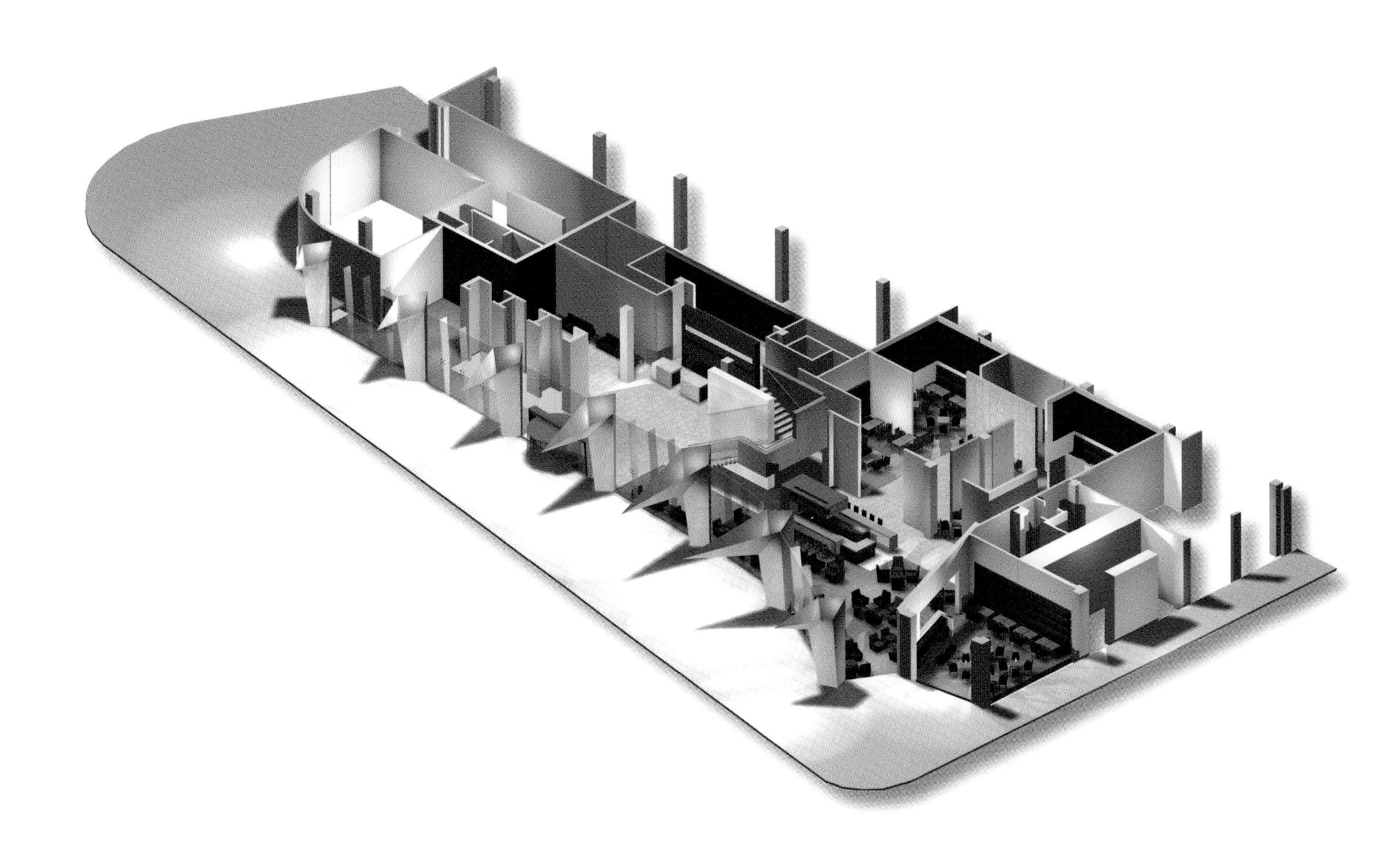

"You look at Radisson, it's a big green façade, but it serves a broader architectural purpose. And the same with Spectrum, there is a reason why that façade bellows out in the way it does. There is a drama and element of quirkiness, but there is also a practical architectural rationale to it." Alan Dunlop

Computer model of the interior.

Design drawings of the bar and lobby area in detail.

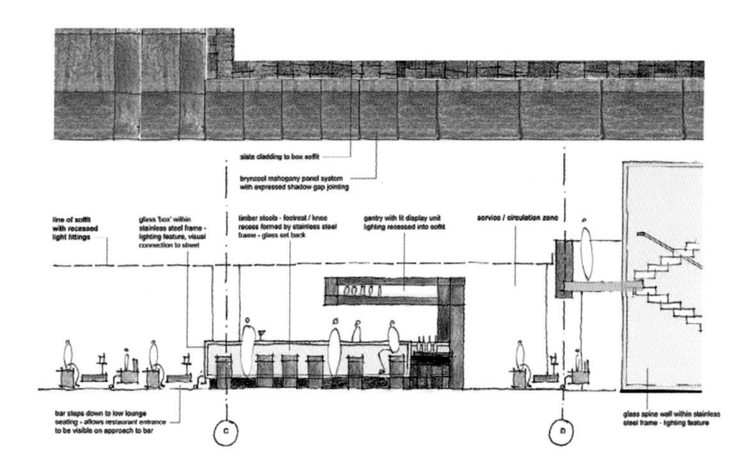

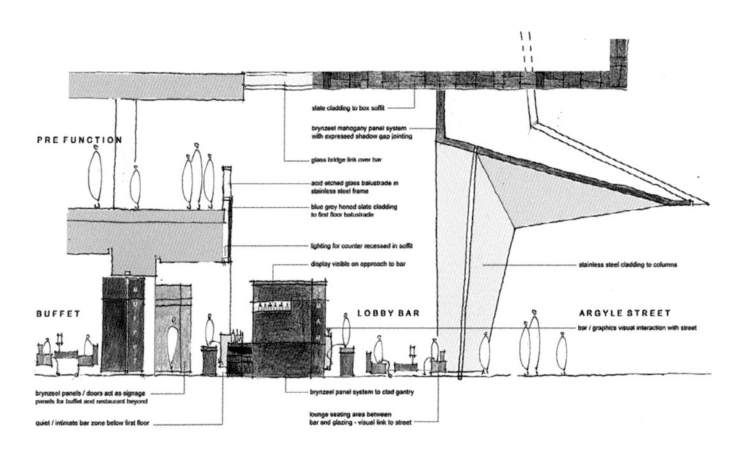

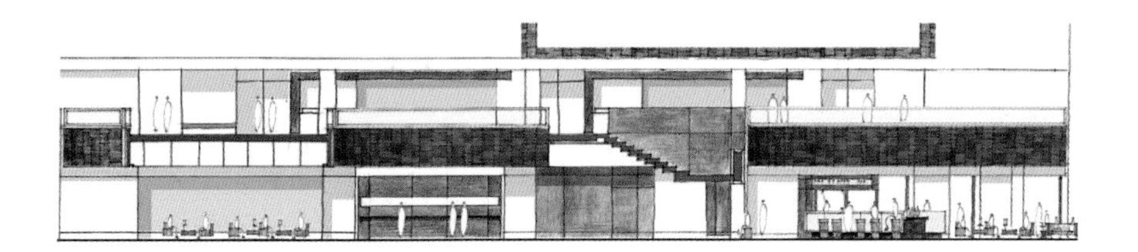

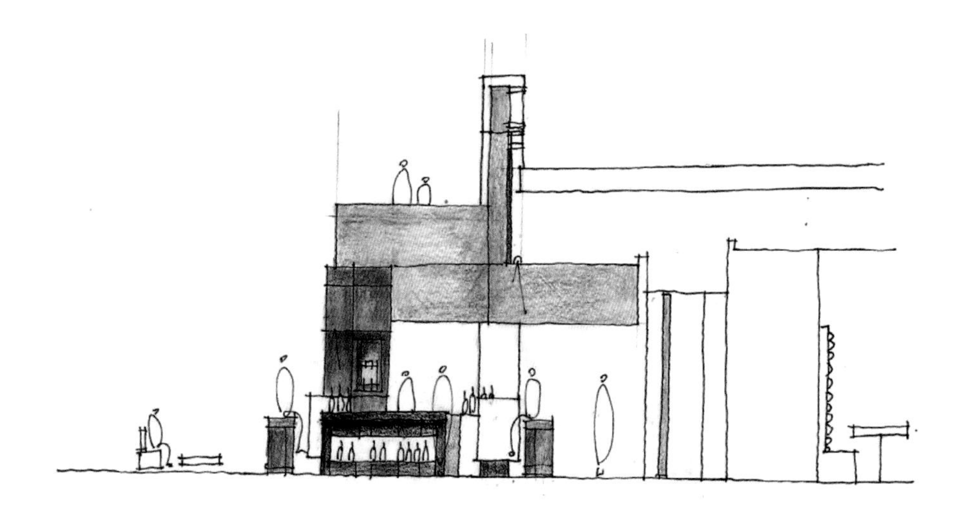

projects

Dunderave

Loch Fyne

IT'S hard to imagine a more spectacular and sensitive rural setting. Dunderave Castle sits on a small headland on the north side of Loch Fyne, four miles north-west of Inverary. The 16th-century castle was elegantly restored by Sir Robert Lorimer.

The current owner of the castle is an enthusiastic art collector and was keen to use some of the land on the estate to build an artists' residence. gm+ad was invited to take part in a limited competition to design the new residence. A collection of old cottages on a sloping site across the road from the castle was identified as a suitable site. gm+ad developed a series of proposals for the site. One proposal was developed for an upside-down house in which the studio and living space were located on the top floor, allowing residents the best possible views of the surrounding landscape. The studio, which cantilevered over the landscape, sat on top of the bedrooms and bathrooms.

Unfortunately, Argyll and Bute planning officials have very conservative tastes and find it hard to appreciate buildings that are not presented with the regulation white render and slate roof. It has also been discovered that the cottages, which are in a derelict state, were designed by Lorimer.

VIEW FROM CASTLE GROUNDS BACK TO SITE

Site plan showing Dunderave Castle and the proposed artists' studio.

Photograph showing the castle.

Early sketches showing different options for the location of the studio.

"I like the idea that poetry and allegory comes in so that you can read things in the building. It's probably a product of spending too much time with Jim Stirling (metaphorically, not literally), that I believe a building should be deeper." Gordon Murray

Model showing proposed studio set among the trees.

Drawings showing elevations and section of the studio that consists of two basic volumes – a workspace on the first floor and living accommodation below.

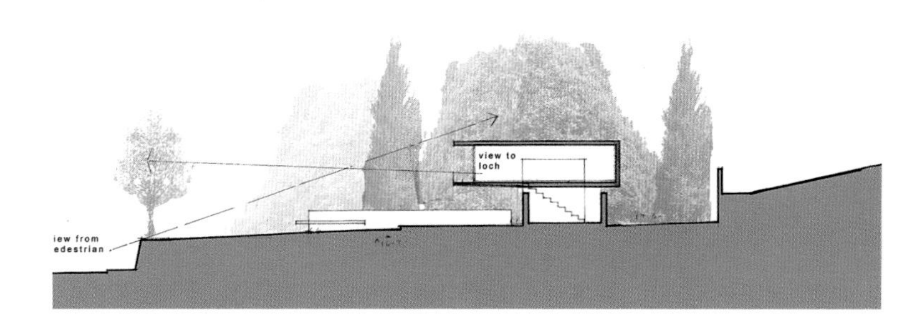

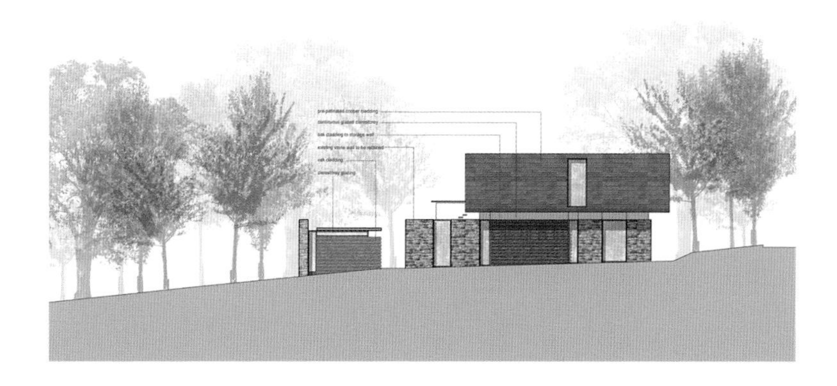

Cheapside

Glasgow

IN June 2002 the practice was appointed by Clydeport/ Glasgow Harbour to develop a master plan for the site, known as Cheapside, to the west of the Kingston Bridge northern approach, which would recognise changing patterns of use and density. The city had appointed Alan Murray Architects to draw up a revised Local Plan for the entire Finnieston area based on earlier strategies which gm+ad had developed to support its River Heights development. The main aims of the master plan were to develop strategies for public pedestrian connections through the site and to create densities that recognised the particularly hostile microclimate in the shadow of the bridge.

In 2005, Dandara, gm+ad's client on Glasgow Harbour Phase 2, appointed the practice to develop plans to full planning consent for all individual buildings and public open space at Cheapside. The uses determined for the site included residential apartments, hotel, offices, leisure spaces and car parking.

Cheapside Street sits in the middle of the site and acts as the area's main public space. East-west routes proposed in the AMA master plan will connect with diagonal routes back to Argyle Street and the international financial services district. gm+ad's ambition is to create a unique public open space under the M8 canopy. Its plans received master plan approval from the city council in 2003. The current scheme recognises the significance of the site as a 'gateway' into the city and its location as a river frontage connecting Finnieston to the city centre. It also sits at an important transport node connecting the low-level railway to the river, the URT system and a new pedestrian footbridge to Tradeston/Kinning Park. The architecture responds to this unique location. The proposals illustrated provide an insight into the development of ideas throughout the project. Planning consent will be sought in spring 2006.

NHS

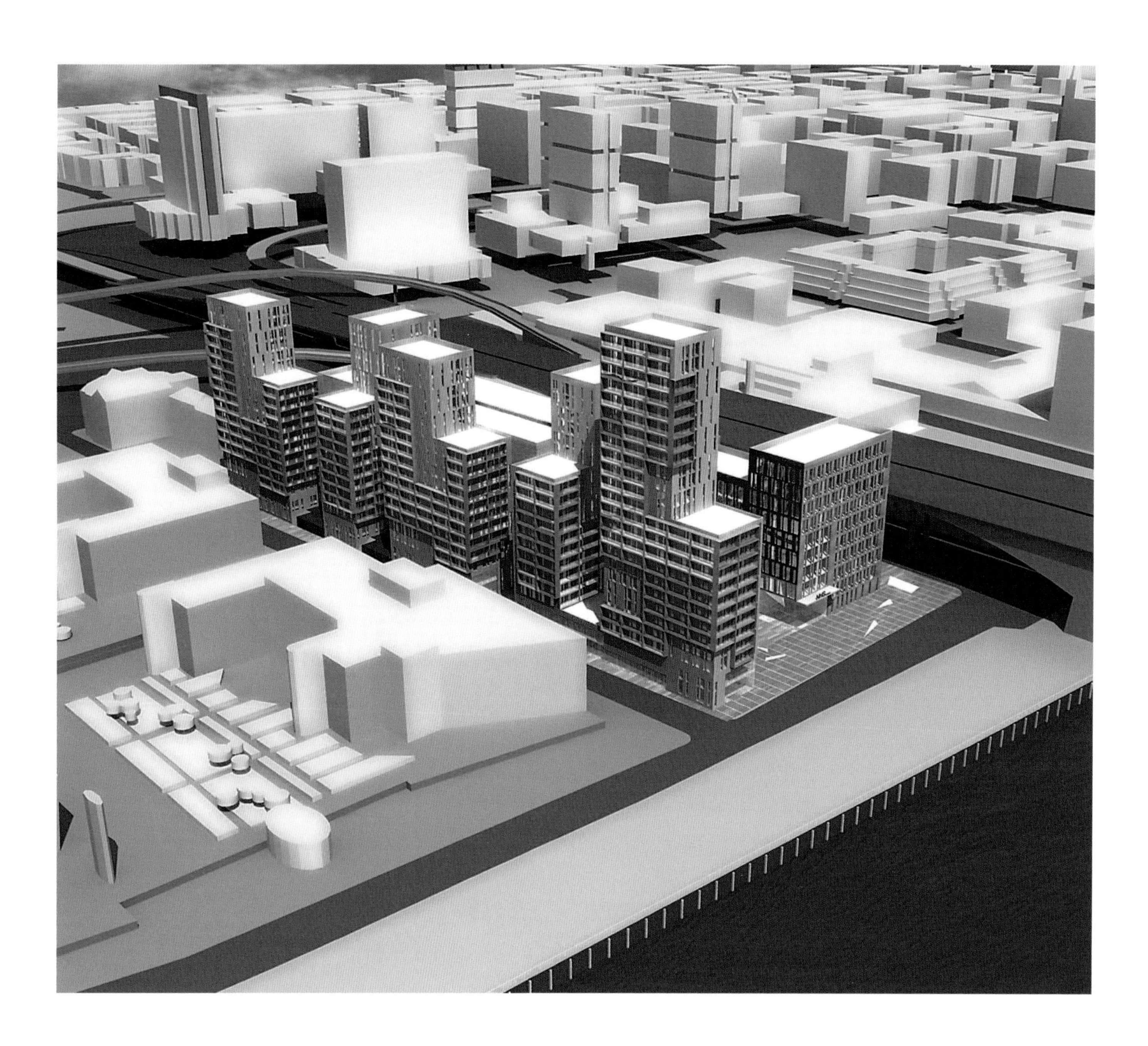

Computer model of the Cheapside form and elevations.

Sketches showing massing of the blocks on Warroch Street.

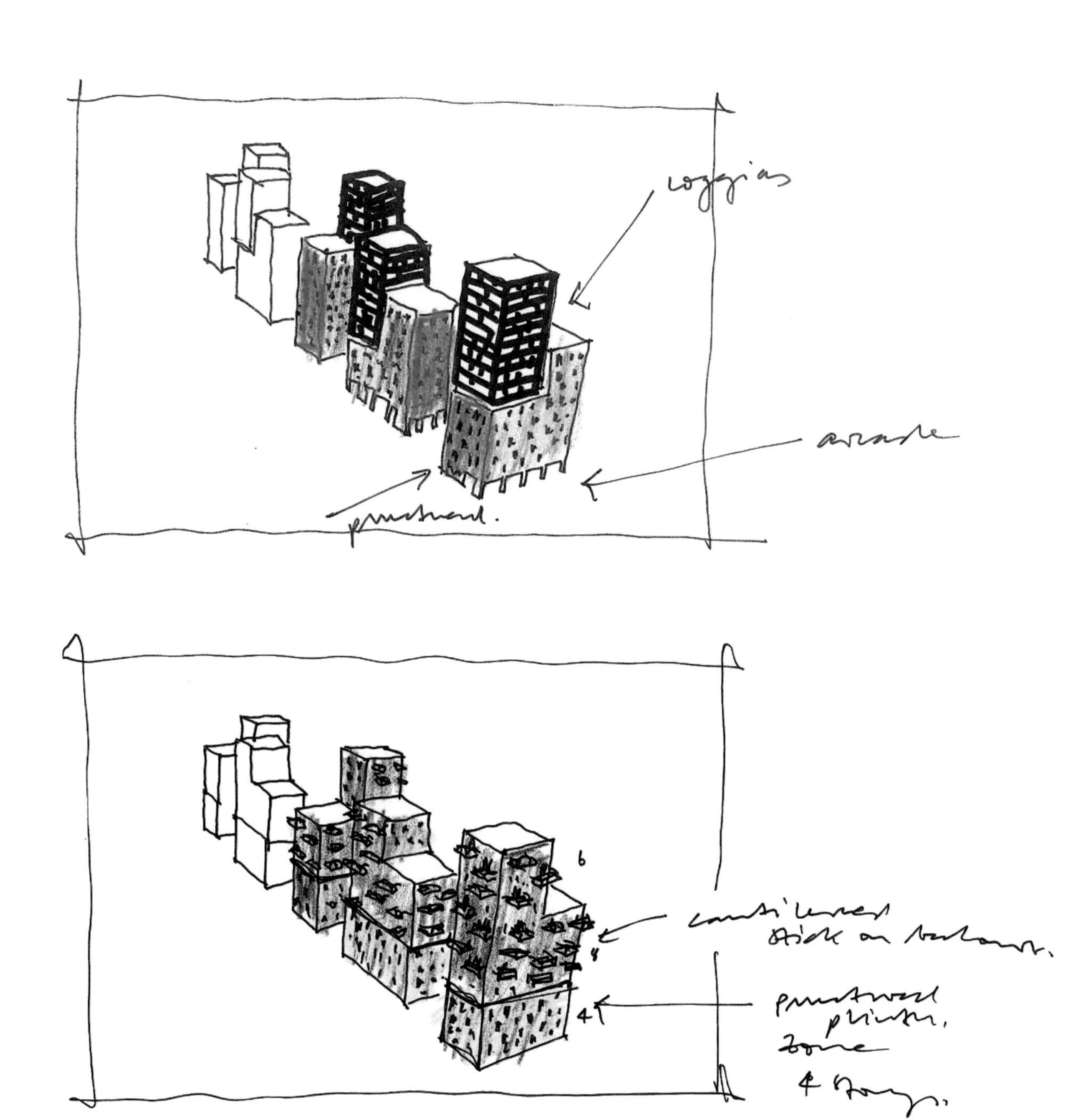

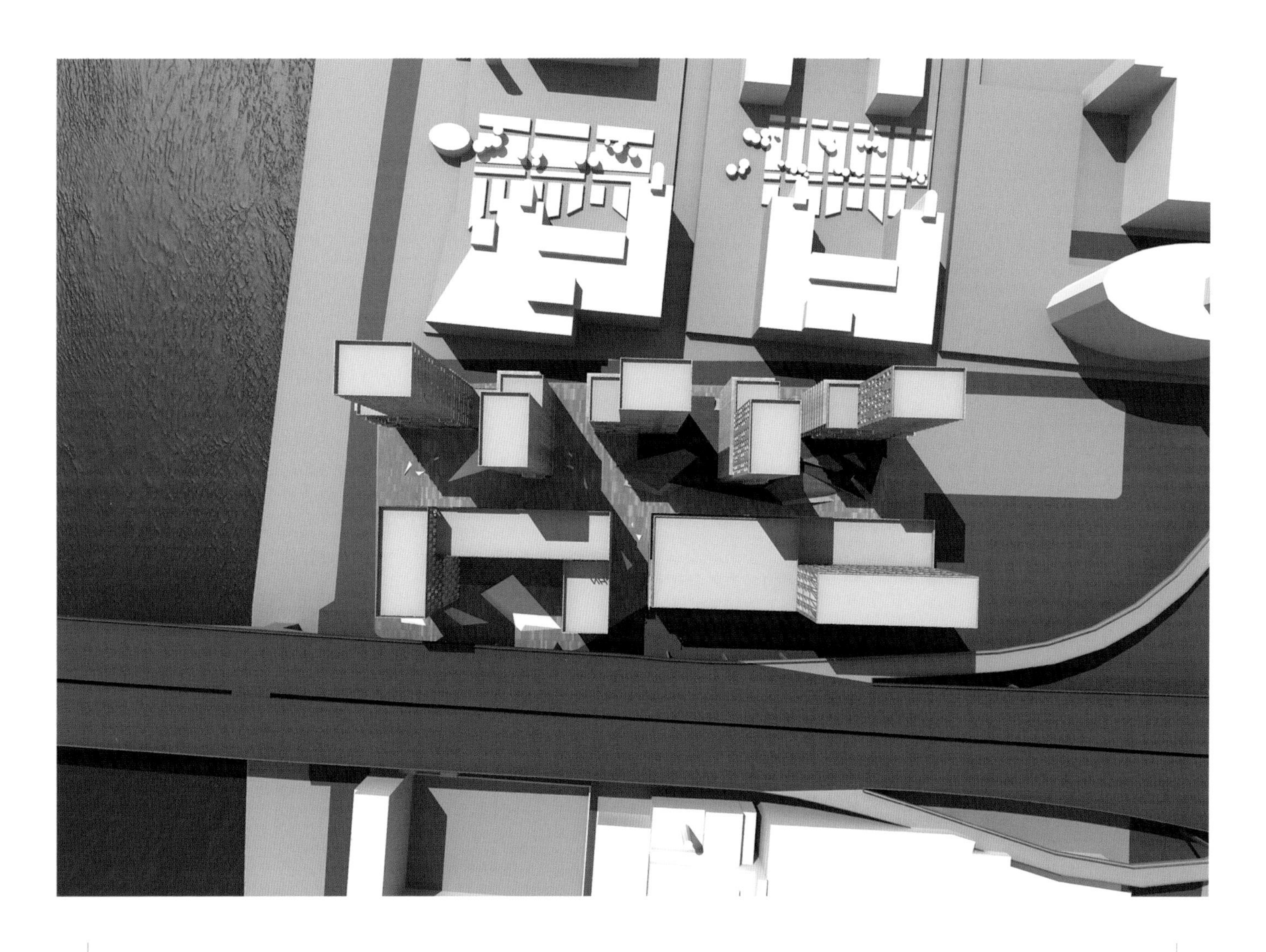

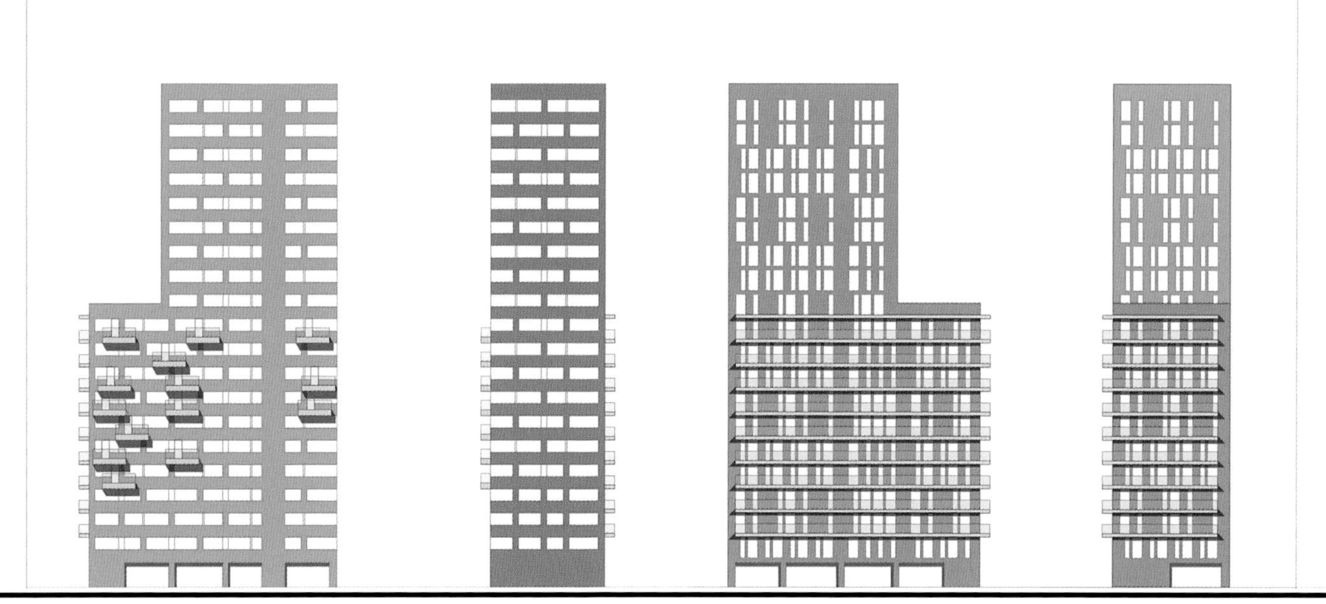

Site plan showing the new public space and pedestrian access across the site.

Design development of the proposed elevations.

Cheapside as seen from the south bank of the Clyde.

The exploration of positive and negative space in the façades of the individual units.

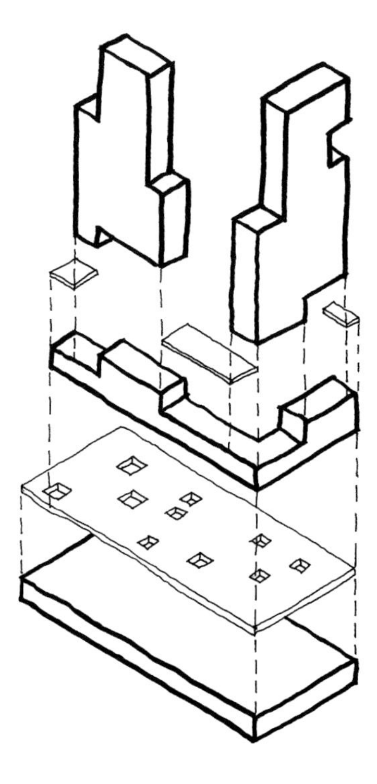

Unicorn Tower

Glasgow

THE client for the project is Mr Jafari, an Iranian who bought the Fazzi franchise, including property on Clyde Street. The building sits in the middle of a terrace on the edge of a conservation area. Before embarking on design work on the Fazzi Building, the practice looked at the entire development of Clyde Street and expressed concerns about the proposed redevelopment of Custom House Quay, which could block river views from the site. gm+ad proposed an alternative plan consisting of a low-lying development in the place of the old sheds and warehouses with a single tower at the Briggait.

In some of the early sketches the Fazzi project was conceived as a building that would be built using a palette of material similar to those on River Heights. However, the practice was keen that a building that stood so close to the new Icon Building by Elder and Cannon should reflect the robust and pared-down character of its neighbour.

When the architects visited the Icon Building they discovered that the wind on the upper balconies was very strong, which inspired them to develop the idea of a winter garden. The winter garden is basically a glazed balcony, which is 1,800mm deep.

The client is a colourful character and the gold gables reflect his personality. The cladding is an anodised aluminium panel, which is powder-coated to give this gold appearance. The architects have not seen the product used anywhere else, but Dunlop cites Hans Scharoun's Berlin Philharmonic with its golden cladding as a source of inspiration. While the building has two golden gables, the main elevation onto the water is glazed; it has frits and colours like a large artwork. The project will provide 53 flats at about 70 square metres each.

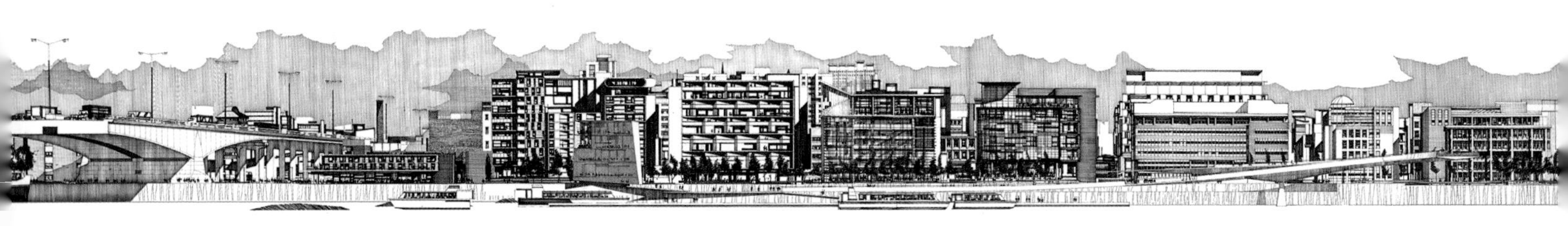

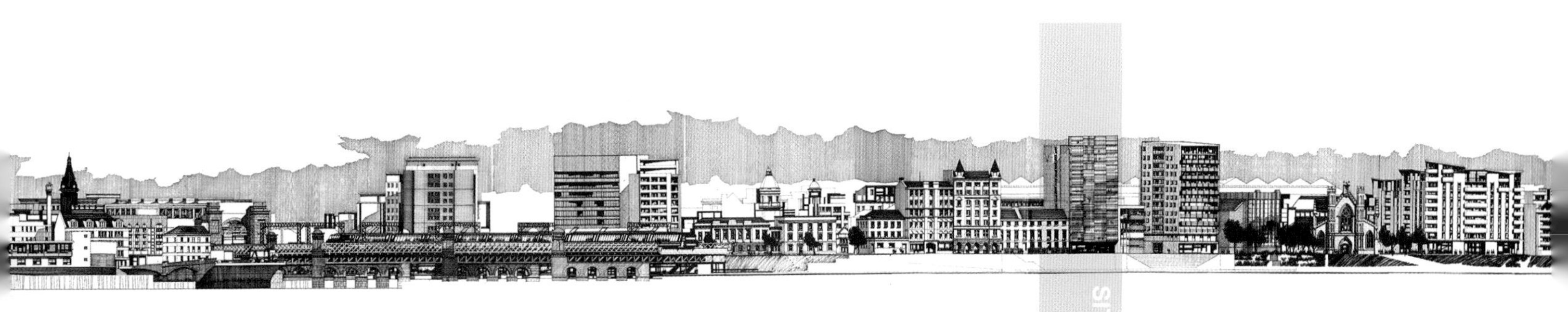
SITE

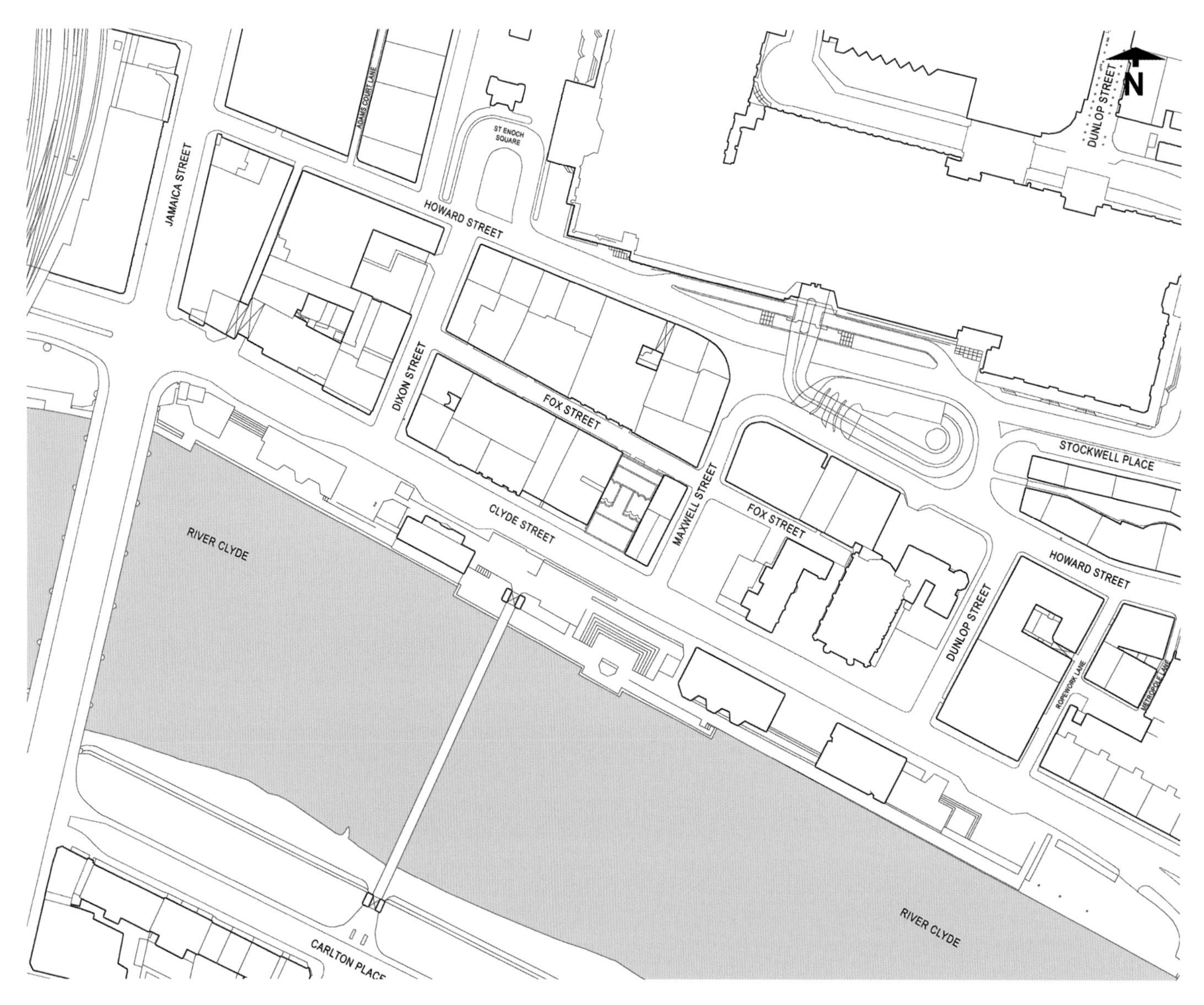
N
JAMAICA STREET
ADAMS COURT LANE
ST ENOCH SQUARE
HOWARD STREET
DUNLOP STREET
DIXON STREET
FOX STREET
STOCKWELL PLACE
MAXWELL STREET
FOX STREET
CLYDE STREET
RIVER CLYDE
HOWARD STREET
DUNLOP STREET
ROPEWORK LANE
RIVER CLYDE
CARLTON PLACE

Site plan showing Unicorn in relation to other developments on the north bank of the Clyde.

A visualisation of the building in relation to existing buildings and two models of the proposed building showing façade treatment.

South, east and west elevations.

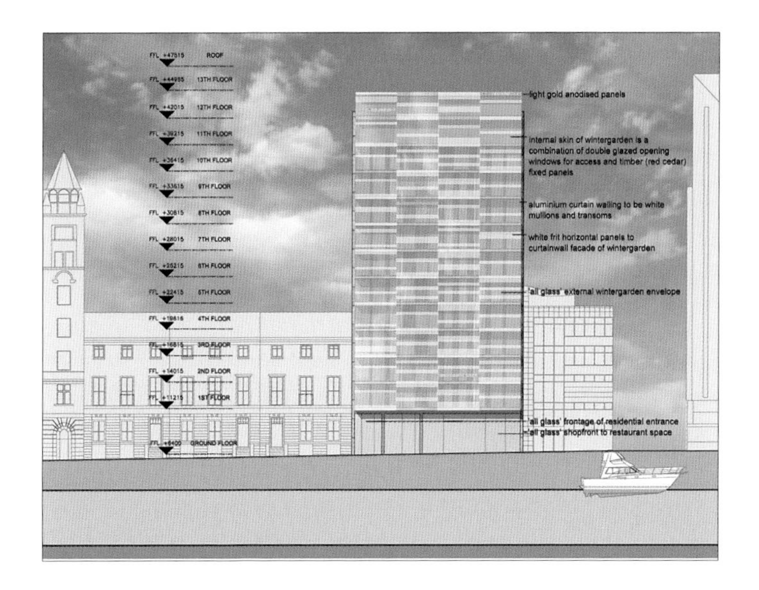

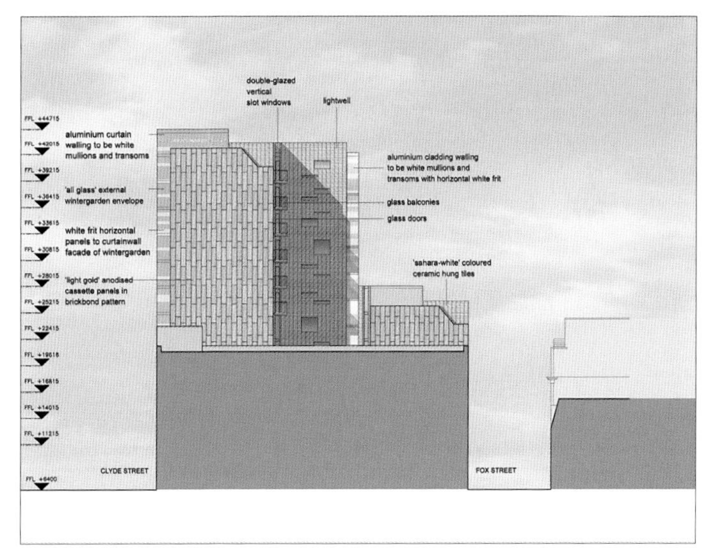

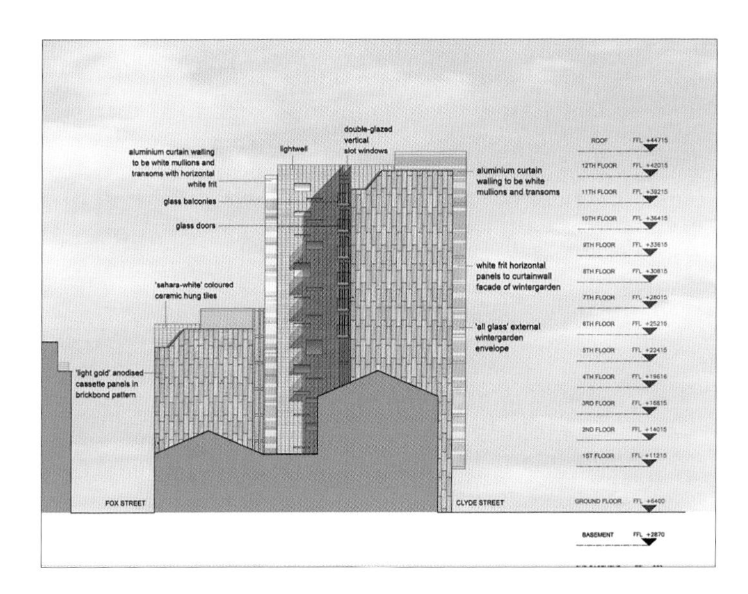

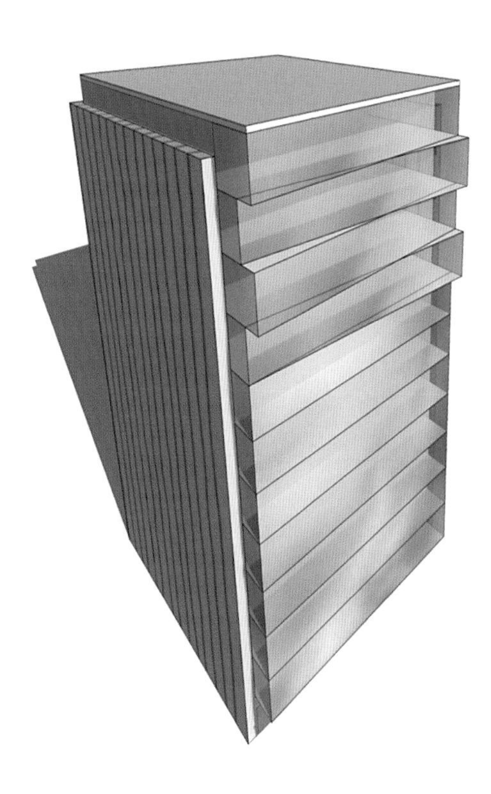

Sligo

Ireland

THIS project would provide a successful case study into the difficulties of getting planning permission in Ireland. gm+ad has recently resubmitted a new planning proposal for the development following a prolonged discussion with the planners and local conservationists. In summer 2003 the practice was asked by Louis Docherty to look at a site from where he ran his antique shop in the centre of Sligo, beside the town's courthouse.

The planning proposals were well received by the council, particularly as they created a series of new routes through the site. Unfortunately, the process of approval became a political football in the local council elections and a local conservationist group, which must be consulted as part of the planning process, insisted that the old buildings must be retained on the site to provide a genuine historic context for the courthouse. A planning consultant was then employed to look at the entire area and make an assessment as to what should be kept, and decided to keep all historic buildings and to restrict new development to a certain height. At this point the architect and client lost interest in the scheme, but have been encouraged recently to resubmit their application. The scheme is progressing in tandem with a local developer responsible for the adjacent site to provide a coherent urban regeneration of this historic part of Sligo. The development consists of four new-build blocks ranging from six storeys down to three storeys with flexible retail/commercial units at ground-floor level and approximately 12 to 15 residential apartments on the upper levels. Parking is provided at basement level and is accessed via the adjoining site. It is intended that the new build will provide a sympathetic link to the proposed refurbishment of the existing listed building, which will also add to the provision of retail/commercial accommodation. The proposed buildings respect the surrounding grain and fabric apparent within the existing townscape, both in scale and materiality, highlighted in the common use of natural claddings such as stone and timber combined with the vivid coloured renders. This development will provide a gateway to the urban regeneration envisaged for this area and it is expected to cost about £2.6 million to build.

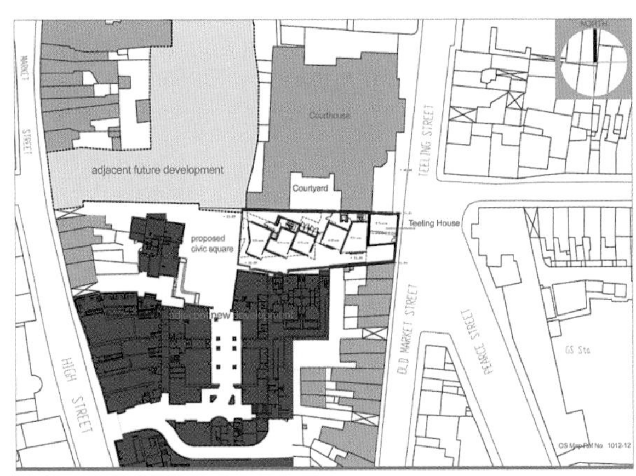

COURTYARD

Hope Street

Glasgow

THIS stretch of Hope Street is a major one-way vehicular route from the river and IFSD to Central station. It is probably one of the busiest parts of Glasgow with 24-hour activity, from commuters, shoppers or people socialising at the numerous pubs and nightclubs. The site is located on the western side of Hope Street and facing the Central Station Hotel and is bounded on the south side by Atlantic Chambers, a Grade A-listed office building dating from 1899 by JJ Burnett. The site consists of two halves incorporating 67 Hope Street, which was originally an eight-storey office and printing works and has a B-listed façade dating from 1899 and designed by Robert Thomson, and a three-storey extension to this building at 65 Hope Street dating from 1933.

In recent years it has been a nightclub at ground and first floor, with the upper floors left to deteriorate. The intention of gm+ad's client is to refurbish and upgrade the existing office space within 67 Hope Street, infill an existing internal light well and create new office accommodation above the nightclub at 65 Hope Street.

From street level, the office building will have a separate identity to the nightclub. An 'all glass' frontage opens into a three-storey-high void containing the vertical circulation and reception. Above this, a glass curtain wall façade will extend to eight storeys, with the uppermost set back in line with its neighbours' roofscape. The intention is that this simplicity of detail will complement and not compete with the ornate listed façades of its neighbours.

Drawing of Hope Street.

The glazed atrium following the line of its neighbours' roofs.

Montages of the proposed building.

Calton Road

Edinburgh

THE Calton Road site is situated towards the east end of the historic 'fish-bone' street pattern of Edinburgh's Old Town. Historic maps of the site record uses including glassworks manufacturing, which has obvious connections to brewing, the only other main industry occupying the Canongate at this time. Later maps show the subdivision of the original burgess 'toft' into narrower width tenemental plots or gardens. By the late 19th century, industrial premises, in the form of the Panmure Foundry, had again occupied the site.

Throughout all of these changes, the site has retained a strong built form defining the corner of Lochend Close and Calton Road. Linear buildings and roofscapes continue this pattern of containment along the historic 'north back of the Canongate', reinforcing the north-south emphasis of the medieval close pattern.

In response to the rich context, an ad-hoc collection of smaller scale elements are pushed and pulled across the width of the site. Reflecting a rhythm and scale analogous to that of the Old Town, this breaks down the overall mass of the proposed commercial building. A six-storey wedge is twisted over the corner of the site and acts as a new visual marker, or reference point, on the pronounced bend in this historic route.

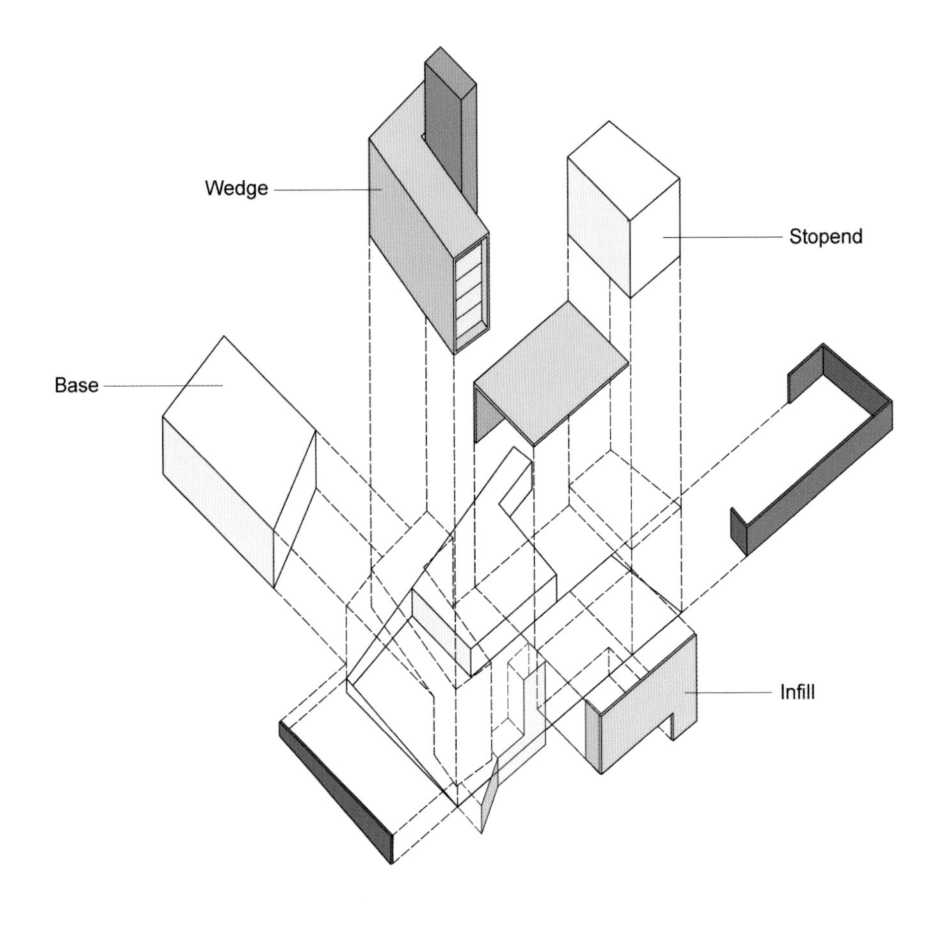

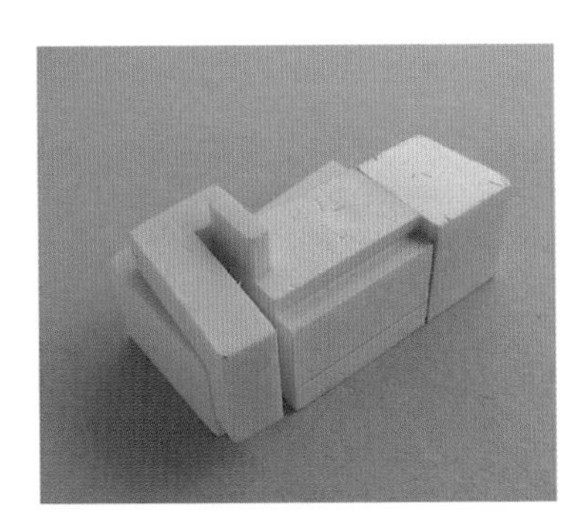

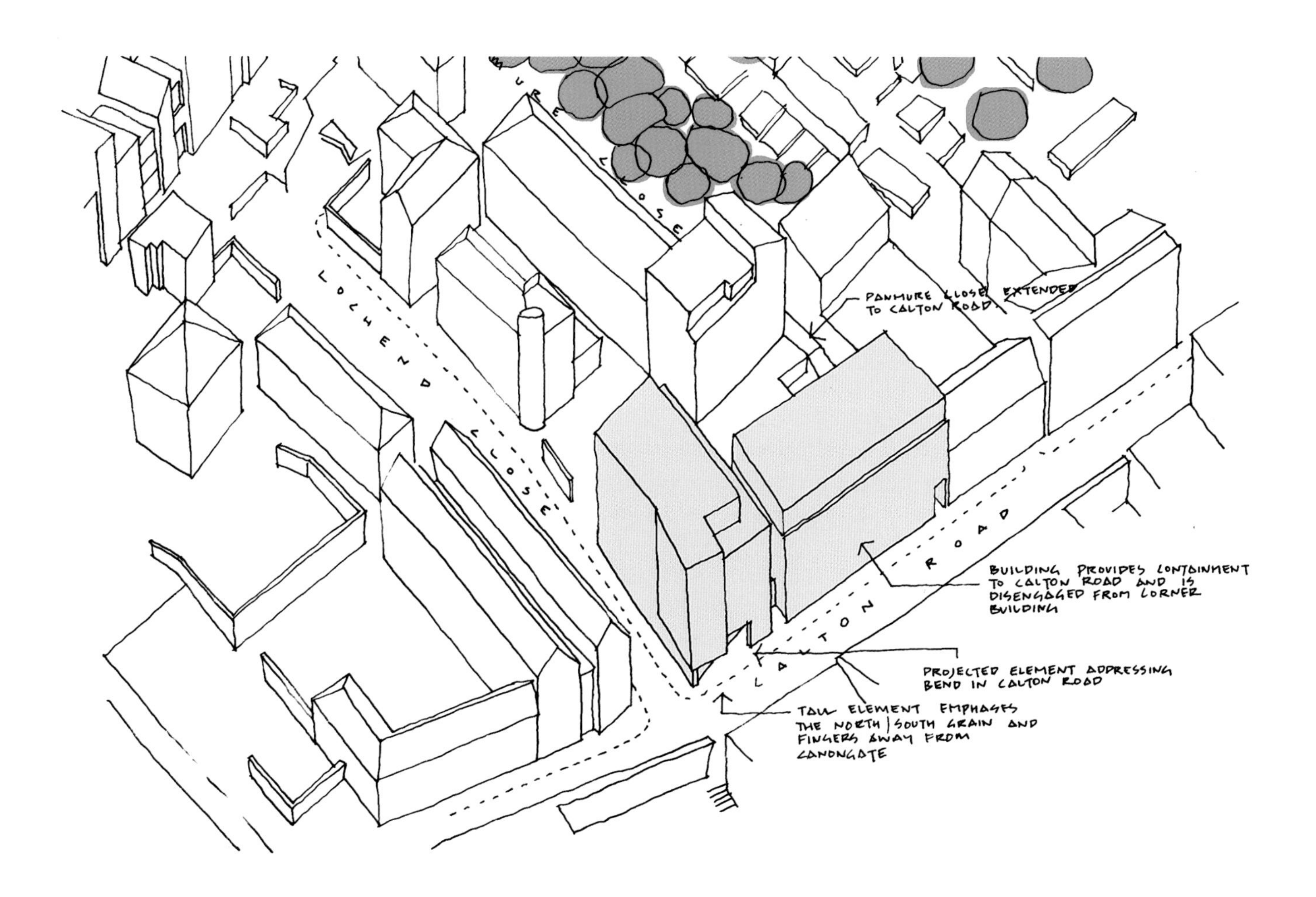

Diagram showing the conceptual approach to the design.

Sketches of the proposed building within the Old Town.

Telford Road

Edinburgh

THE practice was approached by EDI in 2002 to look at a phased residential development that could act as a catalyst for the regeneration of a strip of disused railway land behind Telford Drive in Edinburgh. Most of the existing adjacent housing stock was owned by Manor Estates Housing Association, which, in conjunction with Canmore Housing Association as development agent, became the client for the project.

The site backs onto one of Edinburgh's proposed tram routes and initial ideas included a combination of key worker housing for EDI and social housing units for Manor Estates, together with the integration of a tram stop. This proposal was developed to become three phases of housing grouped around a central landscaped 'street'. The intention from the start was to encourage, through the architecture, social engagement between the various groups of residents. Phase One, which comprises 20 flats, a mixture of one and two-bedrooms in a terraced block, is nearing completion. The buildings have been designed to adapt to the varying needs of the residents over their lifetime with the integration of several fully accessible flats on the ground floors and flexible layouts above.

An important design consideration was how to maintain a sense of privacy and ownership while creating opportunities for interaction between neighbours. The main block is made up of four 'towers', which cantilever off the first-floor podium and begin to define external spaces below. The stair cores are generous with extended glazed landings, which begin to encourage the residents to use them as conservatory spaces. At the first floor, outdoor terraces form shared multipurpose spaces and provide semi-private areas between flats. Each flat has staggered projecting window seats or winter gardens, which open up to southwest-facing balconies.

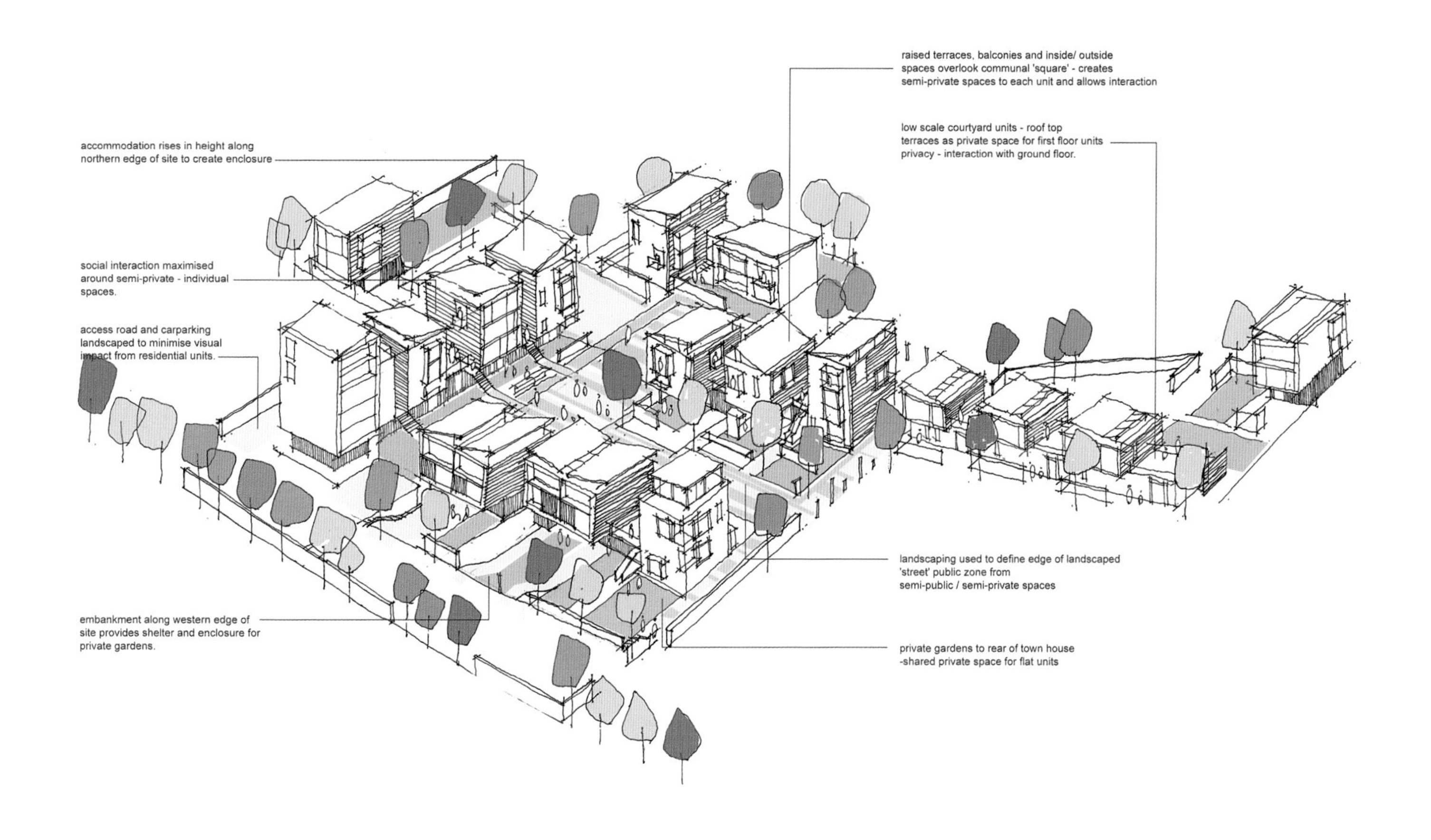

Early concept sketch showing residential units clustered around landscaped social spaces.

Phased masterplan showing mixture of flatted developments and family townhouses.

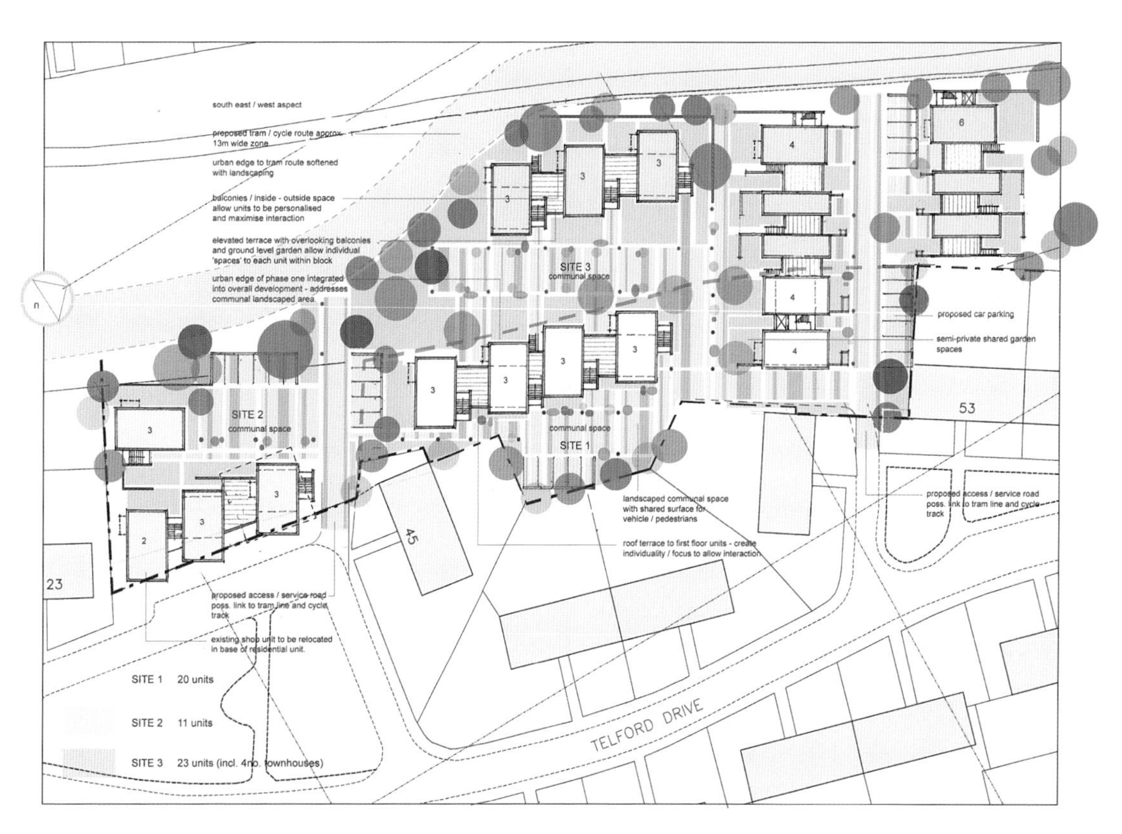

Cumbernauld

North Lanarkshire

CUMBERNAULD was a project in the history of urban design in Scotland and recognised as such by the American Institute of Architects in 1967. The RS Reynolds Award for Community Architecture citation as "the most significant contribution to the art and science of urban design in the western world" was only made possible by those radical powers presented by the New Town legislation.

Cumbernauld town centre sits on the ridge and upper southern slope of the hill above the original village. It rises like a single citadel structure, half a mile long, 200 yards wide and up to eight storeys high. Elevated over a one-directional vehicular system, this multi-level development designed by Geoffrey Copcutt provided for most of the commercial, civic, religious, cultural and recreational uses for a population of 70,000.

Analysis of the original drawings (held in a factory archive on the edge of the town) reveals a beautiful clarity of intention, a megastructure in which nurseries, a library, a social club, welfare and support organisations, a hotel and town squares were brought together.

Forty years later the vision has been horribly compromised. The town has to deal with changing patterns of retail uses, local government administration and welfare provision. Most of the public-sector jobs have disappeared – the remainder are now on the edge of the town centre – and many of the support facilities in leisure and recreation have moved elsewhere. Later developments were located at the four corners of the arterial route and these new retail boxes turn their back on the original centre and existing pedestrian traffic routes.

gm+ad took part in a workshop to look at ways in which the centre could be reclaimed for the pedestrian. Using the concept of habitable public space to mitigate the effects of these anonymous blank façades and car parks. The team suggested restoring a more traditional pattern of high street and vennels, typical of most of Scotland's small towns. The spaces created between these public routes and the existing buildings could, as a result, be added to by further investment, thus increasing the permeability and accessibility of the existing centre, in turn encouraging small businesses. A grid of pedestrian routes at ground level would in turn connect a sequence of public spaces focused on the existing relatively new public buildings located along the southern edge of the town centre. By reintroducing these edges and encouraging activity at ground level space, new possibilities for investment are created. The proposals also suggested the insertion of new leisure facilities into the existing megastructure to encourage people to use the centre outside of the normal shopping hours.

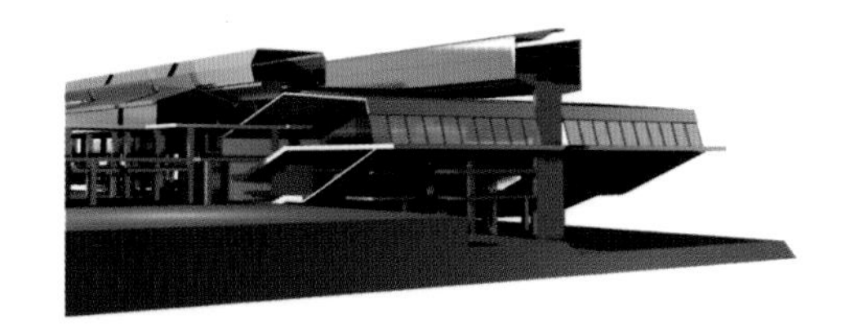

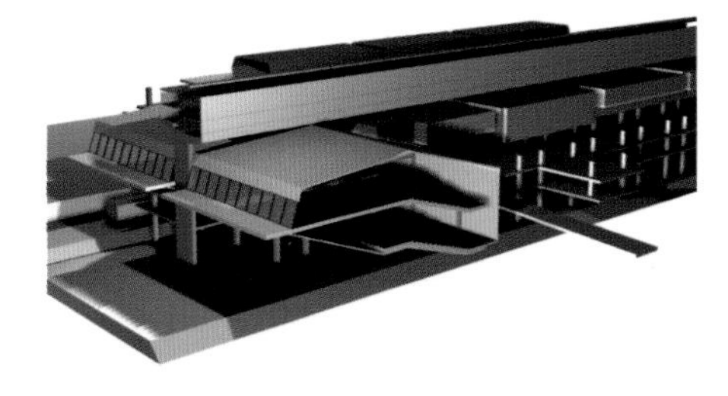

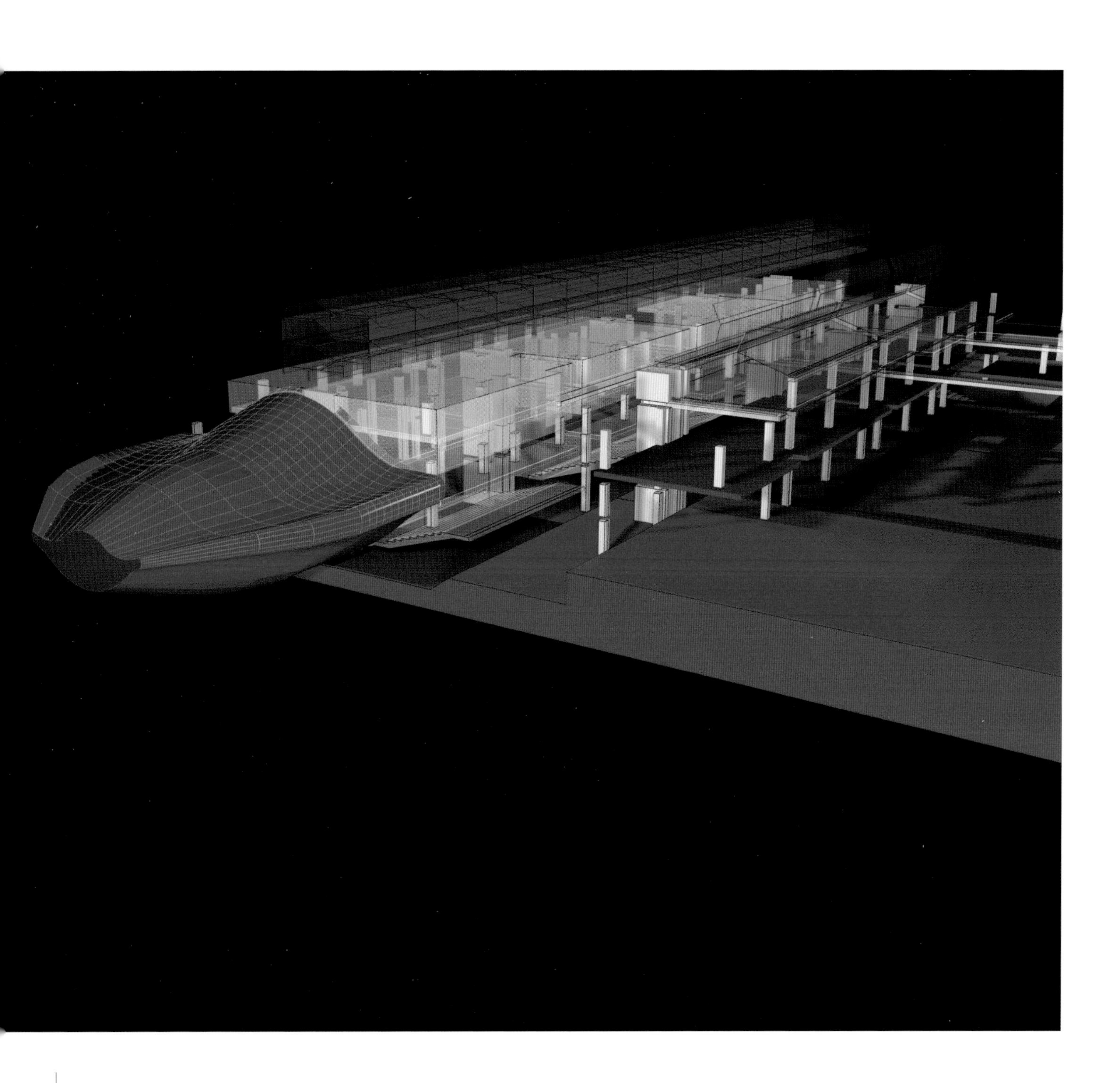

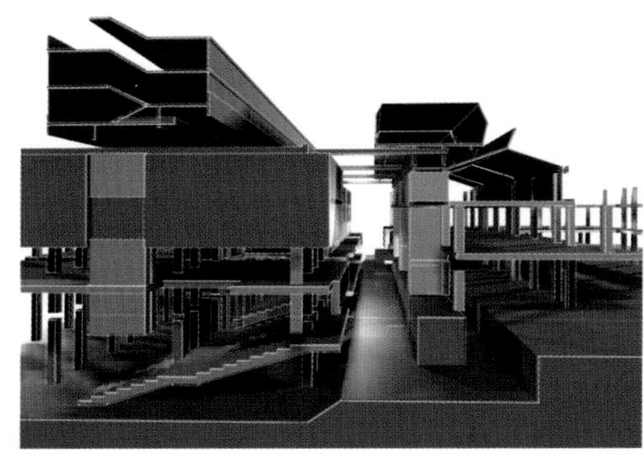

Computer generated images of proposals for the regeneration of Copcutt's original town centre megastructure.

Tradeston Bridge

Glasgow

IN 2004 gm+ad was selected as one of a shortlist of six to participate in the high-profile Glasgow Bridge competition for Glasgow. Also included on the list were Richard Rogers, Norman Foster and Future Systems. gm+ad worked on a joint submission with structural engineers Whitby Bird, landscape architects Gross Max and artist John David Mooney.

The intention was to design a bridge that was very restrained, to create a slender, simple structure and avoid the current fashion for highly exuberant bridge structures. The scheme proposes a low-lying supported bridge with an interesting stepped section creating pedestrian routes on more than one level. The competition was won by a team made up of Atkins and Richard Rogers, with a structure that was far more flamboyant than gm+ad's low-lying proposals.

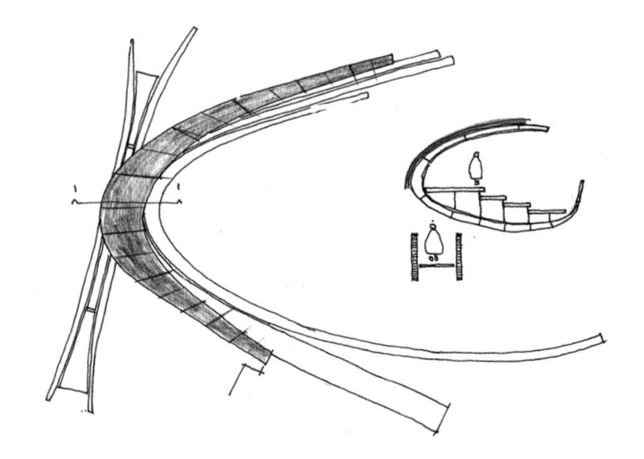

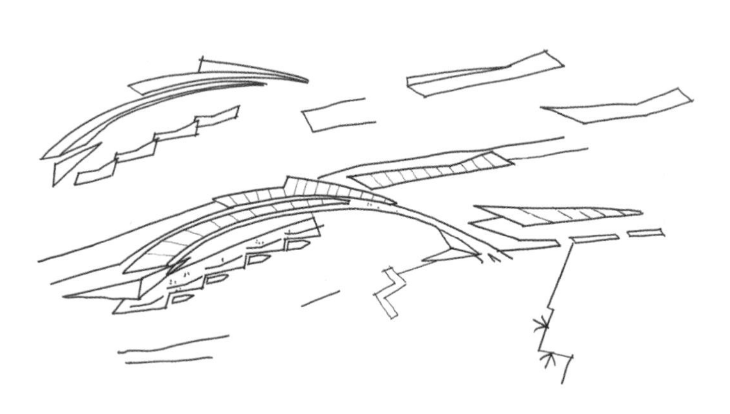

Early sketches showing the attempt to create a bridge form that could offer protection from the weather and a resting place for the public.

The proposed bridge in context.

A section through the bridge showing the folded timber surfaces and level changes.

An image demonstrating the landscape proposals.

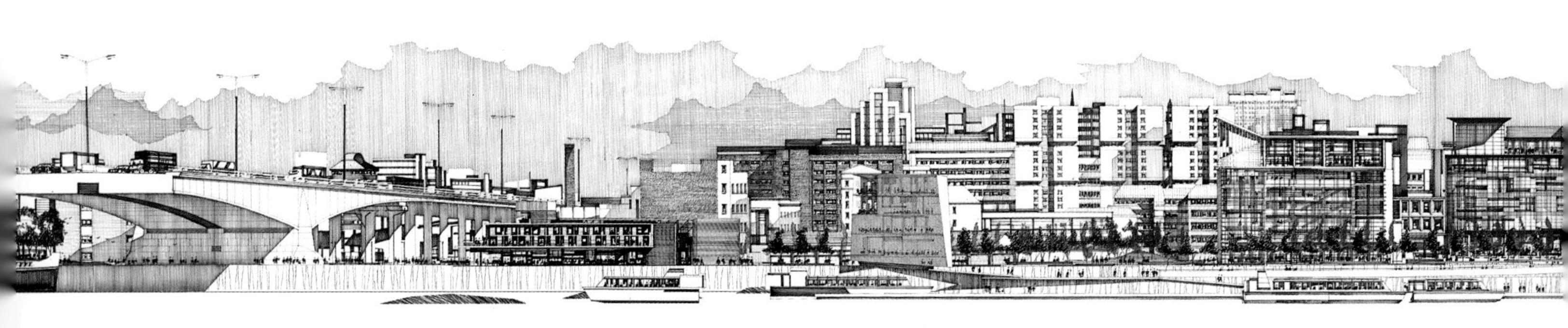

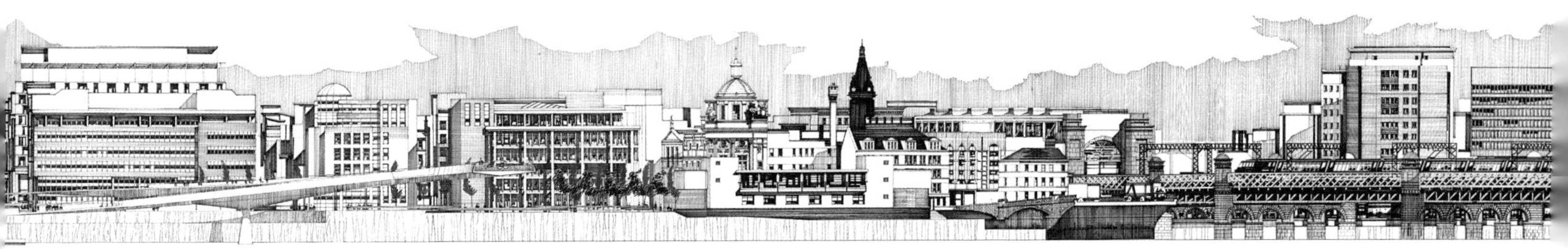

Cardiff Bridge

Cardiff

THE practice responded to an OJEU notice for a car and pedestrian bridge on Cardiff Bay and was one of four practices invited to participate in the competition in early 2005. The other shortlisted practices were Studio Bednarski, Grimshaw Architects and Yee Associates. gm+ad designed a bridge that would say something about the context in which it was built. The bay used to be a tidal water and, as a result, it contains remnants of structures made of timber and steel, built to deal with the old tidal movements. The low-lying bridge has a ship-like section made up of timber and copper elements supported on a carefully engineered and slender spine.

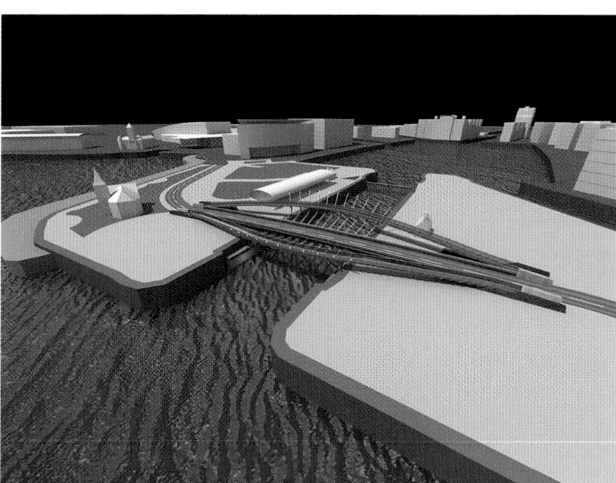

(Not) Black & White

Glasgow

IN summer 2005, gm+ad presented an exhibition of its most recent work in the Review Gallery, a small mezzanine gallery in the Lighthouse (Scotland's Centre for Architecture, Design and the City) in Glasgow. The Lighthouse encouraged the practice to experiment with new ways of presenting architectural material to help the general public engage with the subject and provided a small budget for the exhibition to cover design and production costs.

The aim of the exhibition was to provide an insight into the way the practice works – a view behind the scenes. By using a variety of media – drawings, models and animations – gm+ad hoped to communicate its design ideas and working methods. The gallery sits at the top of an escalator en route to the main exhibitions so the designers felt it was important to produce a show that had a strong visual impact from a distance and would also encourage people to stop and view all the work. A new seat doubles as a plinth for the model displays and the three main elements of the exhibition – the cluster panelled wall, the light box and the curved wall – were arranged around it. The light box displays a mile-long elevation drawing of the Clyde waterfront incorporating two gm+ad projects. An unused existing curved sidewall was painted bright orange and artist Doris Voetter created a signature image for the show on the wall.

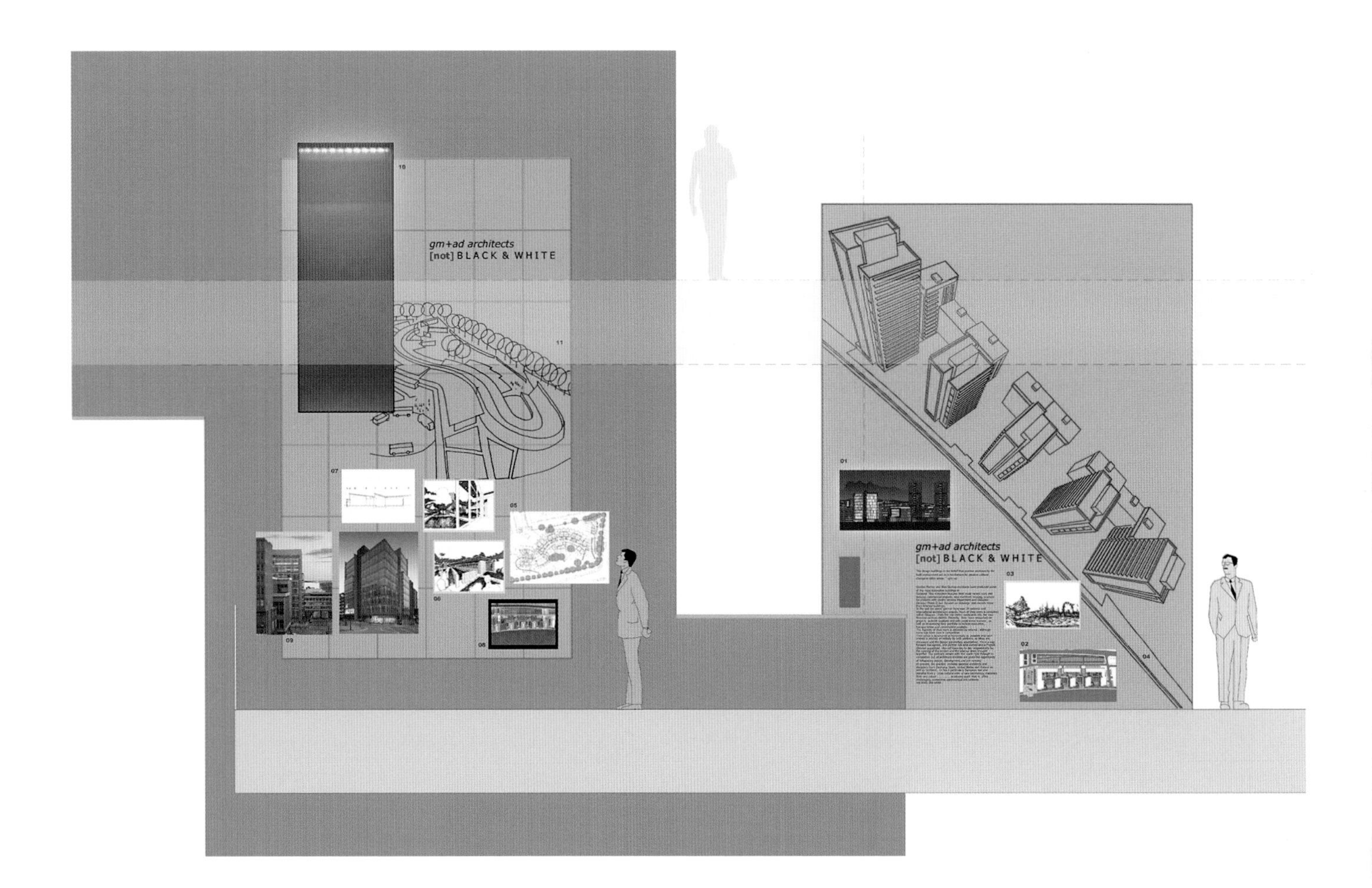

6000 Miles

Glasgow

THE coastal regions of Scotland face a series of significant socio-economic pressures, such as unemployment, social instability, deprivation and market competition. Traditional coastal activities are in decline and concentrated around a few strategic areas along the 6,000-mile coastline, so the indigenous population is changing its relationship with the sea.

To reverse the economic disadvantages of an ageing population and the negative impact of migration, seaside towns will need to develop new activities. Stranraer will lose its status as a significant ferry port in 2006 when the Stranraer to Belfast ferry will be relocated to Cairnryan in order to improve journey times. This move will leave behind a vast pier, a piece of man-made land comparable in size to the town centre.

As part of the *6000 Miles* exhibition gm+ad was asked to look at ways in which Stranraer Pier could be re-used. Its proposal was to cut the pier free from the mainland, reintroducing the pre-ferry coastline of the 1800s. This new channel would then create a series of new waterfronts. The resulting 'islands' would be cut and carved, exposing the historical layering, or memory, of the site, creating smaller islands of various sizes. The people of Stranraer would then reprogramme the pier as an area of land. Each member of this community could contribute in his or her own way, producing an allotment-style development with various functions, from leisure to small-scale business and industry. The result would be a coastal generator or machine, encouraging diversity and providing a unique platform as a socio-economical stimulation.

6000+
30
Welcome to
RANRAER
ase drive carefully

Biennale exhibition

Venice

BOTH Gordon Murray and Alan Dunlop have been campaigning to get Scottish representation at the Venice Architecture Biennale for several years.

After visiting the last Biennale in 2004, Dunlop contacted the British Council to suggest that the 2006 British Pavilion should focus on work taking place outside of London. After an encouraging response from the British Council, Dunlop pulled together a proposal that included the work of leading architects from across the region. They asked Hugh Pearman to curate the show and sent a proposal to the British Council in May. In August they heard that the British Council would be going ahead with the idea of an exhibition focused on work outside of London and that it was running a competition for ideas. The competition was eventually won by Jeremy Till with a proposal to look in detail at Sheffield.

Pearman's proposals would have incorporated the work of gm+ad, Ian Simpson Architects, Glenn Howells, Reiach and Hall and others. Dunlop provided plans and sketches showing how the British Pavilion could be designed to display the works of non-metropolitan architects.

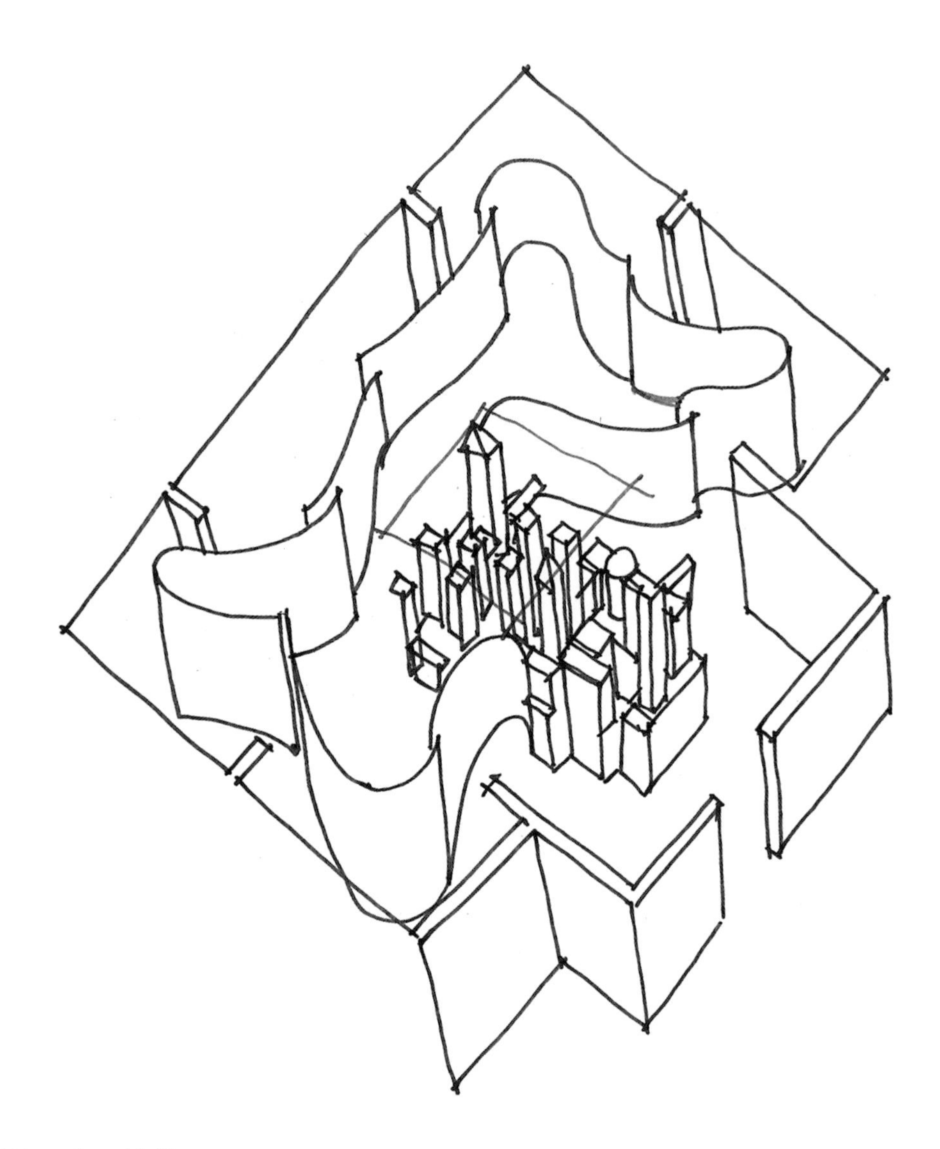

references

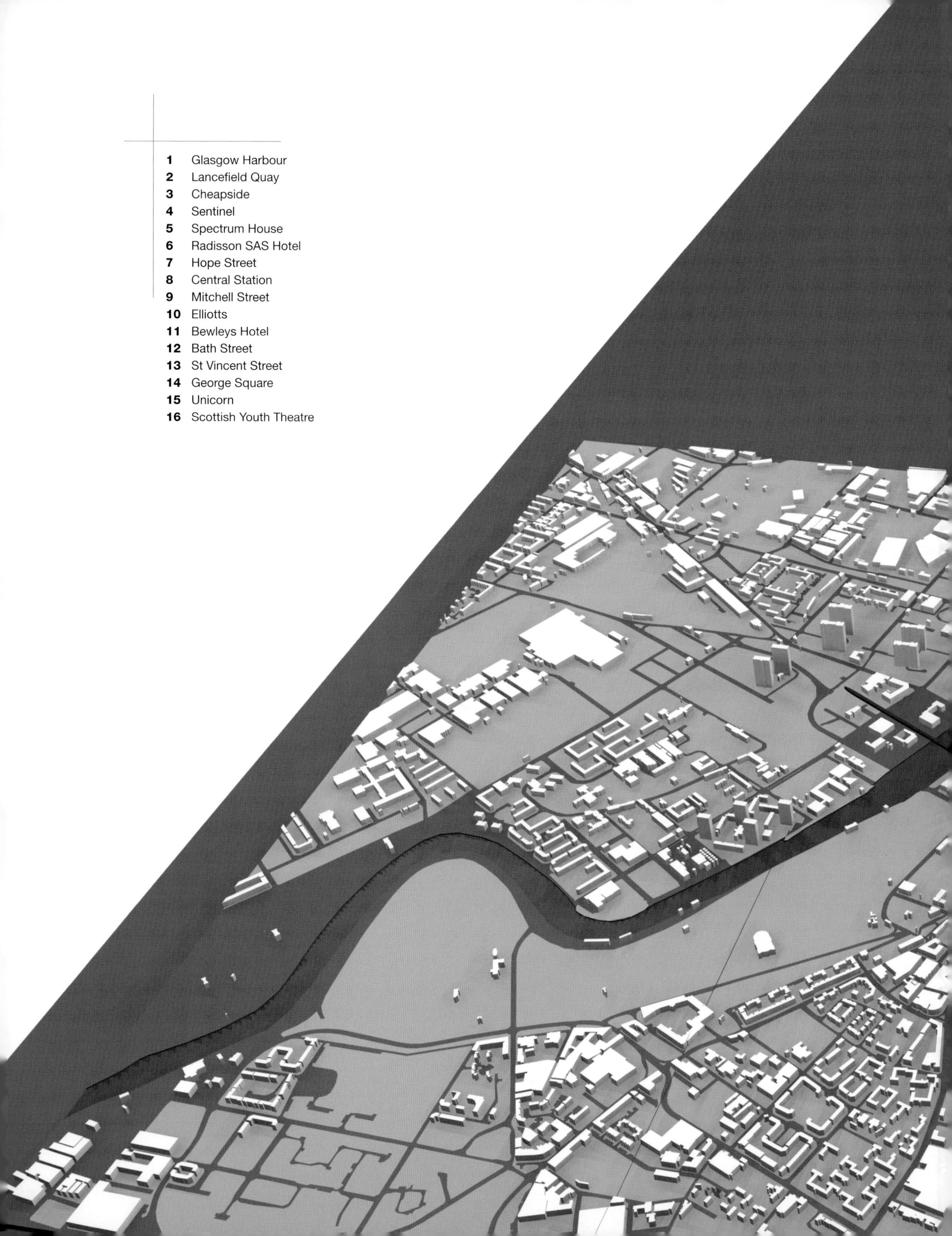

1 Glasgow Harbour
2 Lancefield Quay
3 Cheapside
4 Sentinel
5 Spectrum House
6 Radisson SAS Hotel
7 Hope Street
8 Central Station
9 Mitchell Street
10 Elliotts
11 Bewleys Hotel
12 Bath Street
13 St Vincent Street
14 George Square
15 Unicorn
16 Scottish Youth Theatre

1
2
3
4
5
6
7
8
9
10
11
12
13
14
15
16

Chronology

1996
St Vincent Street
Glasgow

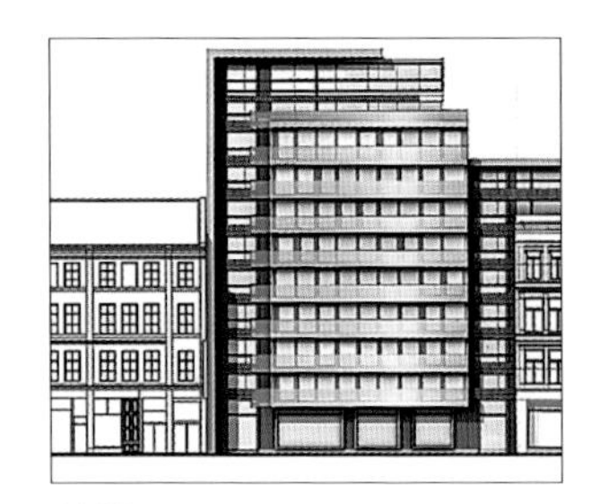

1997
Vienna Apartments
Glasgow

1998
Piping College
Glasgow

1998
George Square
Glasgow

1998
Scottish Parliament
Competition, Edinburgh

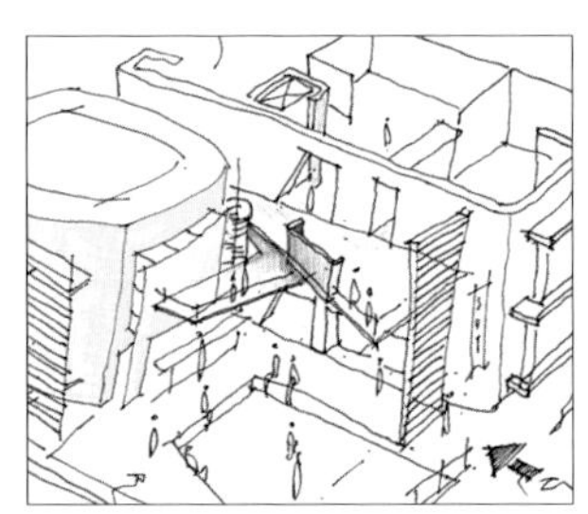

2000
Scottish Youth Theatre
Competition, Glasgow

2000
38 Bath Street
Glasgow

2000
Central Station
Glasgow

2000
Bewleys
Glasgow

2000
Spectrum House
Glasgow

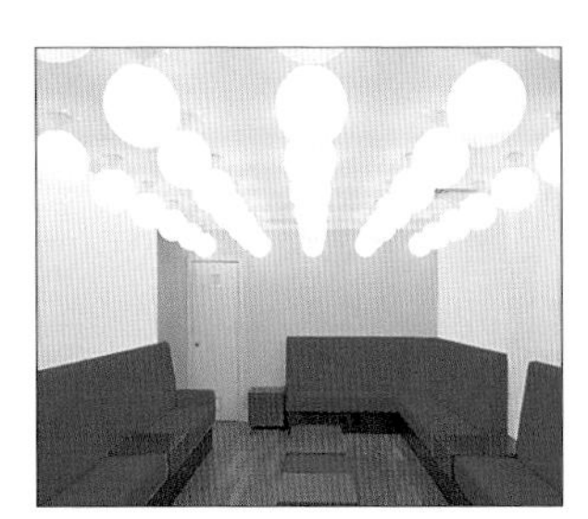

2001
Elliotts
Glasgow

2001
A3
Edinburgh

2002
Crawfurd Theatre
Glasgow

2002
Radisson SAS
Glasgow

2002
Martin Valley Sculpture Park
Competition, Ireland

2004
Sligo
Ireland

2005
Dunderave
Loch Fyne

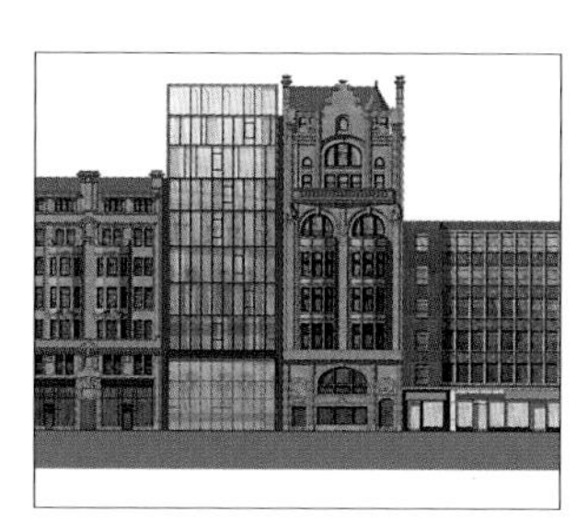

2005
Hope Street
Glasgow

2005
Hazelwood
Glasgow

2005
Sentinel
Glasgow

2005
Tradeston Bridge
Glasgow

2005
6000 Miles
Glasgow

2005
River Heights
Glasgow

2005
Workshops
Clydebank

Staff & Clients

Practice Team

Louise Adamson
Lucy Andrew
Virginia Arbella
Maggie Barlow
Charles Blanc
Saidah Bojens
Mhairi Broadley
Gordon Brown
Sheena Burns
Ewan Cameron
Kate Cullen
Jim Dick
Stephen Doherty
Meg Donegan
Jim Drummond
John Drummond
Alan Dunlop
Markus Elmiger
Ulrike Enslein
Stuart Falconer
Fergal Feeney
Angus Ferguson
David Fleming
Karen Gall
Alison Gallagher
Isabel Garriga
Carlo Guidi
Laura Hart
Kirstin Heger
Lynda Henderson
Elaine Keenan
Robert Kirk
Moritz Korn
James Liebman
Mairi Laverty
Mark Lewis
Sophie Logan
Chris Malcolm
Vivien Mason
Stephen Miles
Andy Millar
Karen Moir
Gordon Murray
Lucie Murray
Philip Murray
Wendy Murray
Heather MacKinnon
Mary McBryan
Katy McKinney
Neil McLean
Graeme McVitie
Diane McWhirter
Shabana Noor
Reiner Nowak
Rory Olcayto
Yeesan Pang
Merrill Park
Stacey Phillips
Mark Philp
Jonathan Pringle
John Rae
Bruce Reid
James Tait
Murray Thomson
Jan Timmermann
Azalee Truan
Ed Wright

This is a list of people who have worked for the practice in the last ten years.

Client list

Arup/London Underground
Ashfield Medical Systems Limited
Atlas Investments Limited
Barratt West Scotland
Bellway Homes
Bett Properties Limited
Bield Housing Association
Care Share Limited
Catren Property Holdings Limited
Child Care (Scotland) Limited
Clackmannanshire Council
Clydebank Re-built
Co-operative Insurance Society Limited
Cordale Housing Association Limited
County Properties Group Limited
Create
Dandara
Danobe Securities Limited
Deaf Connections
Dunedin Property Investment Company Limited
EDI/TIEL
FM Developments Limited
Glasgow City Council
Glasgow Royal Infirmary University Trust
Grampian Country Food Group Limited
Gryff Development Limited
GVA Grimley
HBG Construction Scotland Limited
HBG Developments Limited
Henderson Investors
IBM UK Limited
JP Morgan Chase Limited
Kenmore Property Group
Kilmartin Property Group
Lion/City Lofts
MJ Gleeson Group Limited
Mactaggart and Mickel
Malmaison
Marylebone Warwick Balfour Limited
Medex Medical Inc
Miller Developments Limited
Miller Group Limited
Miller Homes Limited
Morrison Homes Limited
Network Rail
New Edinburgh Limited
North Lanarkshire Council
ProPharma Limited
Radisson SAS
Renfrewshire Council
Safeway Stores Plc
SAS Holdings Limited
Scottish Capital Group
Scottish Enterprise
Scottish Executive
Scottish Postal Board
Scottish Water
Scottish Youth Theatre
South Lanarkshire Council
Spanli Limited
St Martins Property Corporation Limited
Taylor Woodrow Property Company Limited
The Blue Triangle Housing Association Limited
The Burrell Company (Developments) Limited
The Chase Manhattan Bank
The College of Piping
The Scottish Life Assurance Company
The University of Strathclyde
Turnberry Golf and Country Club
Unicorn Developments
Unite Group
University of Glasgow
Venice-Simplon Orient Express Hotels
Welsh Development Agency

Bibliography

Articles by and about gm+ad

Articles by Gordon Murray and Alan Dunlop

'James Miller 1860-1947', Audrey Sloan with Gordon Murray, Royal Incorporation of Architects in Scotland, 1993.

'Clyde Sight', Alan Dunlop, The Scotsman, 29 February 1996.

'Trust the Muse: Refuse to Keep up this Façade',Gordon Murray, The Herald, 1996.

'Six Simple Steps on the Path to Successful Funding', Alan Dunlop, The Scotsman, 1996.

'Constructive Measures Needed to Halt Moral Slide', Alan Dunlop, The Herald, 1996.

'A Short-Sighted Vision', Alan Dunlop, The Herald, 30 October 1995.

'Clarion Call to Focus Attention on River of Change', Alan Dunlop, The Herald.

'Such Riveting Work', Gordon Murray, The Herald, 1996

'The Best Laid Plans', Alan Dunlop, The Scotsman, 27 July 1996.

'A New Beginning', Gordon Murray, The Herald, 7 June 1999.

'Grasping the Thistle', Gordon Murray, Building Design.

'Best Seat in the House', Alan Dunlop, Prospect 2000.

'Manhattan Transfer', Alan Dunlop, Prospect 2000.

'From Small Acorns', Edited by Sandra Wilson and Alan Dunlop, 1997.

'Bringing the City to the River', Edited by Fiona J. Sinclair and Alan Dunlop, 1996.

'The Building Blocks of Life', Alan Dunlop, The Scotsman, 29 June 2001.

'Rebirth of a City', Alan Dunlop, Prospect.

'No Back Corridors',Gordon Murray, The Herald, 1996.

'Acclaim for Hero Hides Ireland's Confidence', Alan Dunlop, Irish Times 9 March 2002.

'A Unique Opportunity', Gordon Murray.

'McCabe: The RFACS Will Soon be Disbanded, But Before It Goes Alan Dunlop Comments on Its Performance', Prospect, April 2004.

'Manhattan Transfer', Alan Dunlop, Prospect, August 2000.

'Bring on the Bulldozers', Alan Dunlop, The Herald, 8 June 2004.

'Greek Tragedy or Demolition Mission?', Alan Dunlop, Evening Times, June 2004.

'Making Waves', Alan Dunlop, Flow Issue 2.

'The Difficult Art of the Simple', Review by Gordon Murray, Prospect, February 2006.

'Third Party Right of Appeal', Alan Dunlop, Prospect, November 2005.

'Sustainability', Gordon Murray, Prospect, 2 February 2004.

'Raising the Game', Gordon C. Murray, Arq (Architectural Research Quarterly), Vol. 6 No. 4, 2002.

'Architectural Research', Gordon Murray, Prospect, April 2005.

'RIAS Award Prize Money', Gordon Murray, Prospect, January 2005.

'Points Win Prizes', Gordon Murray, AJ, 31 March 2003.

'Great Scots', Gordon Murray, Building Design.

'Looking to the Past for a Model of Future City Living', Gordon Murray, The Scotsman, 13 February 2004.

'Il Presidente', Gordon Murray, Chartered Architect, Summer, Autumn and Christmas 2003, Spring, Summer, Autumn, Winter 2004 and Spring 2005.

'European Architecture Policy Forum and Symposium', Gordon Murray, October/November 2005.

'Cynulliad Ceneduaethol, Bae Caerdydd Cymru', Gordon Murray, Prospect.

Prospect R&D, Gordon Murray, 7 February 2005.

'Connecting Criticality?', Gordon Murray, Architectural Review, February 2002.

'Appreciating Cumbernauld', Gordon Murray, Architectural Design, February 2006.

'The Lighthouse: A Centre for Excellence', Gordon Murray, Prospect, 25 September 2003.

'A Life and Architecture', Gordon Murray, Prospect, April 2004.

My Architect, Alan Dunlop, Interview with Nathaniel Kahn and Susan Behr, Prospect August 2005.

Articles and features about gm+ad buildings or about gm+ad or including comments from gm+ad

'Wellington House', Hugh Anderson, AJ, 30 May 1990.

'Black Blueprint', Alan Forbes, The Scotsman, 27 December 1995.

'A Time to Build for the Future', Jennifer Cunningham, The Herald, 9 November 1996.

'A Vision of a Clyde Flowing with Shimmering Vitality', Alistair MacDonald, The Herald, 1996.

'Home Win for Glasgow Architects', Alan Forbes, The Scotsman, 1996.

'New Spirit to Light the Way', Jennifer Cunningham and Carole Ewart, The Herald, 5 October 1998.

'Copper and Glass Luxury', Alf Young, The Herald, 1999.

'Contemporary Glasgow, The Architecture of the 1990s', Johnny Rodger, The Rutland Press, 1999.

'Just the Type', Kenneth Walton, The Herald, 18 March 1999.

'Reductive Criticism', Neil Baxter, AJ, 24 February 2000.

'Scots Bask in Freedom', Robert Booth, Building Design, 1 June 2001.

'Image Building', Stewart McIntosh, Scottish Business Insider, July 2001.

'Full Metal Jacket', Frame Magazine 22, September/October 2001, Spectrum House.

'Hit List', Greg Gordon, The Scotsman, 25 March 2000.

'Breaking Out of the Box', Building Design, 25 January 2002.

'To Build a Better Tomorrow', Claire Prentice, Business AM, 25 June 2002.

'A Tale of Two Skylines', Greg Gordon, The Herald, 29 September 2001.

'Boom Time for Leisure Sector', Bob Serafini, The Herald, 13 February 2003.

'Reconstructive Criticism', Neil Cameron, The Scotsman, 27 November 2001.

'Sitting Target', Greg Gordon, Scotland on Sunday, July 2002, Alan Dunlop.

'Radisson SAS Glasgow', GS Magazine, Autumn 2002.

'Build It and They Shall Complain', Greg Gordon, Scotland on Sunday, 1 September 2002.

'Landmarks Bidding for Top Award', Amanda Eleftheriades, Evening Times, 12 May 2003.

'Spanish Imposition', Radisson SAS Hotel Restaurant Review, Sunday Herald, March 2003.

'Welcome Break', Barrie Evans, AJ, 5 June 2003

'Hotel Scoops Design Prize', AJ, 5 June 2003.

'Originality Breeds Contempt', Katy Archer, The Drum, April 2003.

'Guessing Game of Bridge for Clyde', Tom Gordon, The Herald, 1 November 2003.

'Skyhouse Concept Falls Flat in Glasgow', William Tinning, The Herald, 17 February 2003.

'Scotland the Brave', Austin Williams, 11 September 2003.

'Kelvin Bridge Cannot Span £1m Funds Gap', Phil Miller, The Herald, 11 September 2003.

'Pipes Dream About to Come True', James Doherty, The Scotsman, 11 September 2003.

'One Site for Sore Eyes', Alexander Linklater, The Herald, 2003.

Abstract Magazine 19, June 2003, Radisson SAS.

'A New Image for Tourism', Prospect, February 2003.

'Family Planning: How a Scottish Architect Extended Himself for the In-Laws', Cover, The Sunday Times. 27 April 2003.

'New Kid on the Block', Fiona Armstrong, Homes and Interiors, August 2003.

'Family Planning'
Greg Gordon, The Scotsman Magazine, May 2003.

'Site for Sore Eyes'
Andrew Doolan, Scotland on Sunday Magazine, 21 September 2003.

'Natural Born Hotelier', Darren Gardner, Sunday Herald, February 2003.

'Boom Time for Leisure', Bob Serafini, The Herald, February 2003.

'Bridging the Last Gap', Agnes Stevenson, The Herald Magazine, 25 October 2003.

'Building a Bridge Over the Clyde...', Greg Gordon, Scotland on Sunday, September 2003.

'UK's Best Buildings', The Independent Magazine, September 2003.

'Sligo has an Aspiration', Frank McDonald, The Irish Times, November 2004.

'Full Metal Jacket', Jonathan Glancey, The Guardian G2, 3 March 2003.

'THE BIG DEBATE: Ditch the Listed Building System', The Herald, 15 June 2004.

'Award-Winning Firm to Design Special School', Stephen Stewart, The Herald, 26 May 2004.

'Architects Sent Back to School', Greg Gordon, Scotland on Sunday, 15 February 2004.

'The Winner Takes it All', Alex Linklater, Prospect, September 2004.

'Arhitektura U Svetu', Dans, October 1996. Arq, Vol. 8, No. 2, 2004.

'Green Light Given for City's New School', Kevin Schofield, The Scotsman, May 2004.

'Top Award for Landmark City Centre Office Building', Evening Times, June 2005, Sentinel.

'Out with the Old, In with the New', Magnus Linklater, Scotland on Sunday, 20 June 2004.

'On Road to New Look for National Park', Rob Crilly, The Herald, 12 May 2004.

'Pay Attention Also to What's Being Built', Mario Conti, The Herald, June 2004.

Dumbreck School 'Learning to Live', Anna Chambers, Prospect, December 2004.

'Brickbats for Buildings You Love to Hate', Calum MacDonald, The Herald, 21 August 2004, Spectrum.

'Architect Attacks 'Old-Must-Stay' View of Buildings', Stephen Stewart, The Herald, June 2004.

'Cutting a Dash in Edinburgh', Project Scotland, May 2004.

'Bulldoze 'Em', Jamie Livingston, Sunday Mail, 31 October 2004.

'Architectural 'Holy of Holies' to Feature New Scottish Work', Jim McBeth, The Scotsman, 5 June 2004.

'Second's Out as Firm Builds Its Reputation', Project Scotland, May 2004.

'Tower Plan to Bring Clyde's Glitter Back', Stephen Stewart, The Herald, October 2004.

'Take the High Rise', Greg Gordon, The Sunday Times: Home, 23 January 2005.

'Tower Block Designers Go Back to the Future for New-Look City', Jim McBeth, The Scotsman, 22 March 2005.

'High Life Beckons with 700 Flats in Latest Stage of Plans to Develop City Harbour', Stephen Stewart, The Herald, March 2005, Glasgow Harbour.

'Designed to Make Waves', Mark Fisher, The Herald, 15 March 2005.

'A Ray of Light', Bob Serafini, The Herald, 3 March 2005.

'City to get Europe's Top School for Blind', Gerry Braiden, Evening Times, May 2005.

'Scots Hotels are Better by Design', Craig Brown, The Scotsman, 15 April 2005, Radisson.

'Leading Architect Attacks Glasgow Council', Aideen McLaughlin, The Sunday Herald, April 2005.

'Red Road Row Rubbished', Rory Olcayto, Project Scotland, April 2005.

'Is This Just a Return to 1960s High-Rise Living?', David Leask, Evening Times, 22 March 2005, Glasgow Harbour.

'Contextualism', Penny Lewis, Prospect, June 2005.

'Northern Lights', Stephen Zacks, Metropolis, December 2005.

'The Radical Radisson', Mark Collins, Forma Interiors, Vol. 4 Issue 3.

'Can't Afford a House? Blame Your Parents', Greg Gordon, The Sunday Times, 14 August 2005.

'Work Under Way on Europe's Top School for Blind Children', Chris Musson, Evening Times, 8 December 2005.

'PPP Schools "Little More Than a Roof"', Andrew Denholm, The Herald, 8 December 2005.

'Scots Mall "UK's Worst Eyesore"', Marc Horne. The Sunday Times, 11 December 2005.

'Skills in Demand', Brian Edwards, AJ, 25 August 2005, Radisson.

'Architects Look to Pupils for School Plan', Craig Brown, The Scotsman, 8 December 2005.

'School Building Programme Branded a Waste of Money', Kevin Schofield, The Scotsman, 21 December 2005.

'21st Century Hotel', Graham Vickers, Laurence King Publishing 2005, Radisson SAS.

'Bazaarchitecture!, Project Scotland, August 2005.

'Interview with Gordon Murray', Paper Space (Department of Architecture, University of Strathclyde), 2005.

'Scotland: Quest to Fly Scotland's Housing Flag', Greg Gordon, The Sunday Times, 6 February 2005.

'Get the Most from Your Coast', Peter Wilson, Building Design, 8 April 2005.

'Holyrood Wins Architecture's Oscar', Senay Boztas, Sunday Herald, 16 October 2005.

'Exhibition', Brian Edwards, AJ, 25 August 2005.

'Sketchbook/Alan Dunlop', 'Proposal for the 2006 Venice Biennale', AJ, 12 January 2006.

'Clydebank', Penny Lewis, Prospect, February 2006.

'gm+ad/Clydebank', Neil Gillespie, AJ, 2 February 2006.

Index